James Stirling Michael Wilford & Associates

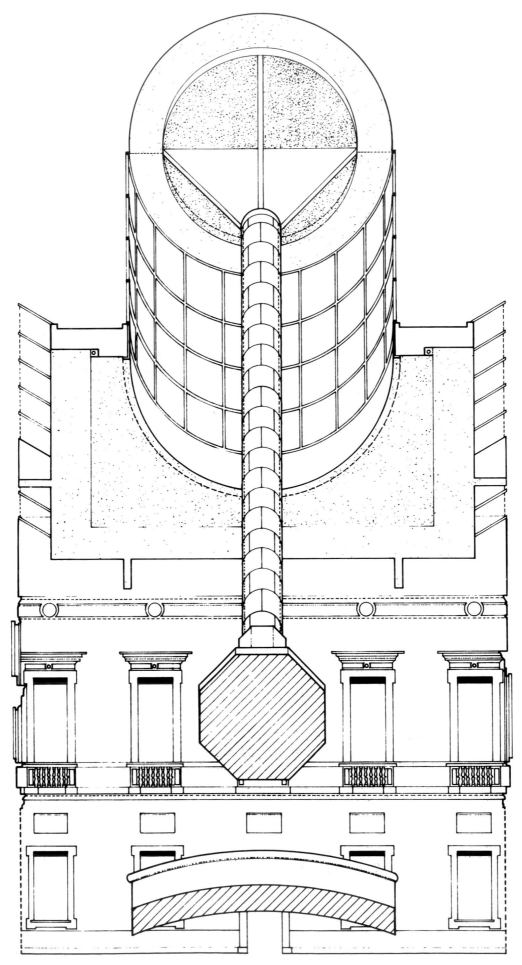

PARTIAL AXONOMETRIC, PALAZZO CITTERIO ART GALLERY, BRERA MUSEUM, MILAN

An Architectural Design Profile

James Stirling Michael Wilford & Associates

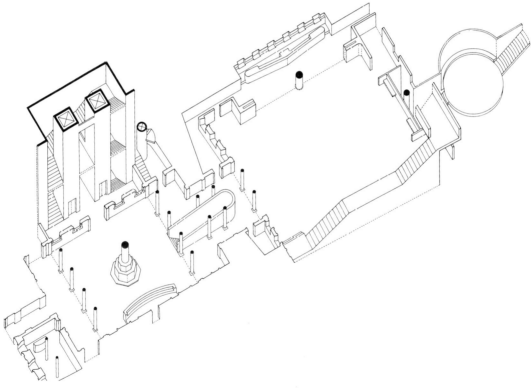

DISSECTED AXONOMETRIC, PALAZZO CITTERIO ART GALLERY, BRERA MUSEUM, MILAN

ACADEMY EDITIONS • LONDON / ST. MARTIN'S PRESS • NEW YORK

Acknowledgements:
This special issue of Architectural Design was prepared in close collaboration with James Stirling. All colour photographs of Cornell University by Richard Bryant. pp 19, 44, 80, 86, 92, 104, model photographs by John Donat. p 40 model photograph by Udo Hesse. pp 28, 32. Models constructed and photographed by Kandor Model Makers.

Credit List for Projects featured in this issue.

Centre for the Performing Arts, Cornell University, Ithaca, New York, USA James Stirling, Michael Wilford, George Gianakopoulos, Robert Dye, Steve Bono, Robert Kahn, Walter Naegeli, Ulrike Wilke, Stephen Bono, Joan Nix, Harry Spring, Leonard Franco, Val Antohi. **Museums For New Art and Sculpture, Tate Gallery, London** James Stirling, Michael Wilford, Richard Portchmouth, David Jennings, Leandro Rotondi. **No 1 Poultry, Mansion House, City of London** James Stirling Michael Wilford and Associates, Laurence Bain, Andrew Birds, Felim Dunne, Michele Floyd, Toby Lewis, Alan Mee, Richard Portchmouth, Peter Ray, Michael Russum, Manuel Schupp. Consultants: Planning Agents: Montagu Evans, Caws and Morris; Quantity Surveyor: Monk Dunstone Associates; Consulting Engineers: Ove Arup and Partners, Jaros Baum & Bolles; Project Manager: Project Direction; Landscape: Arabella Lennox-Boyd; Letting Agents: Baker Harris Saunders, Hiller Parker. **Thyssen Art Gallery, Villa Favorita, Lugano** James Stirling Michael Wilford and Associates, Russell Bevington, Ulrike Wilke, Paul Barke, David Jennings. Structural and Services Engineers: Ove Arup and Partners; Quantity Surveyors: Davis Belfield and Everest. **Braun Headquarters, Melsungen, West Germany** James Stirling Michael Wilford and Associates in association with Walter Naegeli, Alois Albert, Annegreg Barg, Ludger Brands, Hans-Georg Conradi, Renate Keller, Thomas Kemmermann, Matthias Konsgen, Hella Rolfes, Norberto Schornberg, Renzo Vallebuona, Gretchen Werner, Siegfried Wernik. **State Theatre Warehouse, Stuttgart** James Stirling Michael Wilford and Associates, Ulrike Wilke, Paul Barke. **Bracken House, London** James Stirling Michael Wilford and Associates, Laurence Bain, Paul Barke, Desmond Burne, Ulrike Wilke. Structural and Services Engineers: Ove Arup and Partners; Quantity Surveyors: Monk Dunstone Associates. **Kaiserplatz, Aachen, West Germany** Marlies Hentrup and Norbert Heyers with James Stirling. **Palazzo Citterio Art Gallery, Brera Museum, Milan** James Stirling, Michael Wilford, Tom Muirhead, Russell Bevington, Oliver Smith, Toby Lewis, David Jennings, Philip Smithies, Michael McNamara, Ove Arup and Associates. **New Opera House , Glyndebourne** James Stirling, Michael Wilford, Laurence Bain, Andrew Pryke, Charlie Hussey, Ulrike Wilke. Costs: Gardiner and Theobald; Acoustics: Derek Sugden; Theatre Consultant: John Bury. **Science Library, University, Irvine, Los Angeles** James Stirling Michael Wilford and Associates with IBI/L Paul Zajfen, California, Peter Ray, Richard Portchmouth, Mike Russum, Felim Dunne, Chris Chong, Eilis O'Donnell, Toby Lewis, Buddy Maer, Ken Hetherington, Barbara Helton-Berg, Mark Tannin, Katherine Ware. Structural and Mechanical Engineer: Ove Arup; Cost Consultants: Adamson Associates; Library Consultant: Nancy McAdams. **Residential Development, Canary Wharf, London** James Stirling, Michael Wilford, Russell Bevington, Toby Lewis, Michael McNamara, Thomas Muirhead, Eilis O'Donnell, Steve Proctor, Philip Smithies, David Turnbull and YRM PLC. **Los Angeles Philharmonic Hall, Los Angeles** James Stirling, Michael Wilford, Russell Bevington, David Turnbull, Luigi Ferrara, Christopher McCormack, Eilis O'Donnel, Toby Lewis, Michael McNamara, Philip Smithies, Martha La Gess, David Jennings, Charlie Hussey, Michael McCann. Acoustics Consultants: Arup Acoustics; Sructural Consultants: Ove Arup and Partners. **Stadium Development, Seville** James Stirling, Michael Wilford, David Turnbull, Charlie Sutherland, Chris Dyson, Mike Russum, Andrew Birds, Leandro Rotundi, Charlie Hussey, Ove Arup and Partners. Associate Architects: GTP Seville. **Compton Verney Opera House** James Stirling Michael Wilford and Associates. **Bibliothèque de France** James Stirling, Michael Wilford, Russell Bevington, Toby Lewis, Manuel Schupp, David Jennings, Eric Yim, Andrew Pryke, Charlie Sutherland, Chris Dyson, Catherine Martin, Paula Blyth-Lewis. Structural and Mechanical Engineers: Ove Arup and Partners; Quantity Surveyors: Gardiner and Theobald. **Biennale Bookshop, Venice** James Stirling Michael Wilford and Associates, Tom Muirhead. **Tokyo International Forum, Tokyo** James Stirling, Micheal Wilford, Takashi Yoneyama, David Turnbull, Charlie Hussey, Charlie Sutherland, Yashumiro Imai, Hideo Saijo, Eric Yim, Jun Nakano, Tom Muirhead, Eilis O'Donnal, John Bowmer, Steffen Lehmann. Engineers: Ove Arup and Partners.

EDITOR
Dr Andreas C Papadakis

EDITORIAL OFFICES: 42 LEINSTER GARDENS, LONDON W2 3AN TELEPHONE: 071-402 2141
HOUSE EDITOR: Maggie Toy DESIGNED BY: Andrea Bettella, Mario Bettella SUBSCRIPTIONS MANAGER: Mira Joka
CONSULTANTS: Catherine Cooke, Dennis Crompton, Terry Farrell, Kenneth Frampton, Charles Jencks
Heinrich Klotz, Leon Krier, Robert Maxwell, Demetri Porphyrios, Colin Rowe, Derek Walker

First published in Great Britain in 1990 by *Architectural Design*
an imprint of the
ACADEMY GROUP LTD, 7 HOLLAND STREET, LONDON W8 4NA
ISBN: 1-85490-042-0 (UK)

Architectural Design Profile 85 is published as part of *Architectural Design* Vol 60 5-6/1990
Published in the United States of America by
ST MARTIN'S PRESS, 175 FIFTH AVENUE, NEW YORK 10010
ISBN: 0-312-05562-5 (USA)

Printed and bound in Singapore

ACCESS GALLERIA, THYSSEN ART GALLERY, LUGANO, SWITZERLAND

Contents

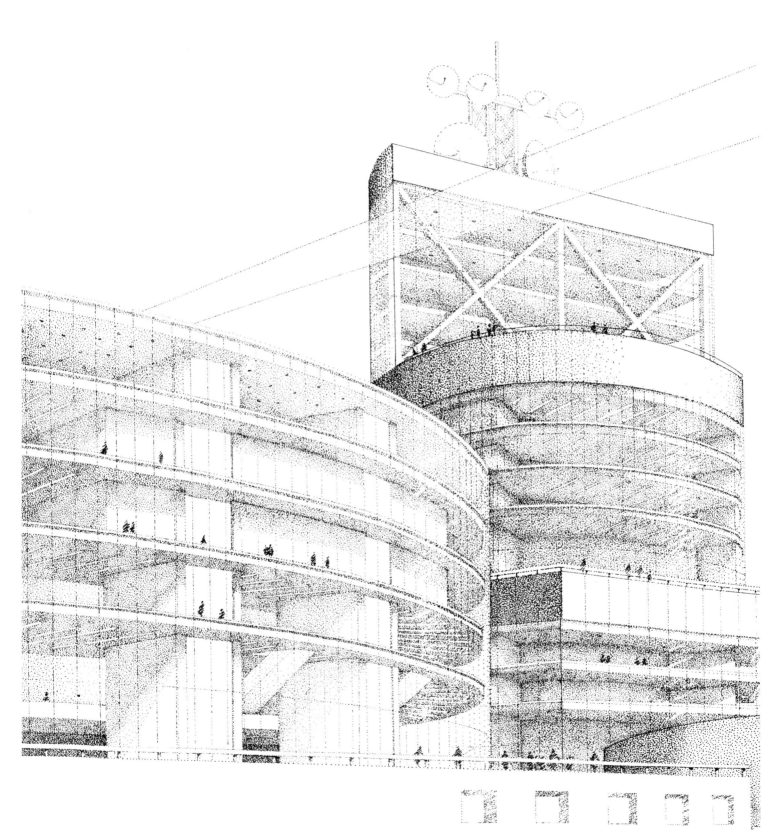

PERSPECTIVE VIEW, TOKYO INTERNATIONAL FORUM, TOKYO

JAMES STIRLING
DESIGN PHILOSOPHY AND RECENT WORK

VIEW OF ENTRANCE HALL, BIBLIOTHEQUE DE FRANCE, PARIS

I have always maintained that our designs 'emerge inevitably', from a logical analysis of the site, together with a functional interpretation of the programme, emerging as it were, 'hey presto'. Nevertheless, there is a certain 'formalism' and 'style' in their built appearance. Looking back, it is the realisation that our designs have sometimes come in 'series', which leads me to think that we have

a stronger 'formal expression' than I previously would have admitted. A style appearing in 'one' project could be an accident, and in 'two' might be a coincidence, but when it reappears in 'three' must surely be deliberate.

There were for instance, our three University buildings of the 50s and early 60s - The Engineering department at Leicester, the history faculty at Cambridge and the student residence at Oxford - all variations on a theme, all low cost buildings, comprised of industrial glazing, engineering bricks and external tiles. Lack of 'care and maintenance' has resulted in them now looking rather sad. In England, these buildings have suffered an ideological fall from grace, victims of the swinging change of fashion. From being regarded as heroically *avant garde* in the early 60s they are now regarded as alien and malformed. Our future King has likened modern architecture to a carbuncle on the face of society.

I am not sure why designs come in 'series', although it is characteristic of some architects' work, for instance Frank Lloyd Wright's concrete block houses in Los Angeles and Le Corbusier's early studio houses in Paris. These architects were able to keep moving on to later 'series', with all manner of 'one-offs' in between.

But coming down to my level, the projects of Richard Meier or Robert Stern, for instance, are always brilliantly consistent, that is mainly repeats. I console myself with the view that our

production, whilst a good deal more eclectic, is, I think, more appropriate in the current 'evolutionary' phase of modern architecture.

Our work has oscillated between the most 'abstract' modern (even High-Tech), such as the Olivetti training school, and the obviously 'representational', even traditional, for instance the Rice University School of Architecture. These extremes have characterised our work since we began, but significantly, in recent designs (particularly the Staatsgalerie), the extremes are being counter-balanced and expressed in the *same* building.

Prior to 1970 our buildings were mainly in the semi-private category - schools and university buildings - often in green field or suburban sites. It is only with the more recent museum designs that our architecture has, I hope, become positively civic and populist.

In 1975 we were invited to take part in two competitions for museums in West Germany. The German government had, with post-war reconstruction, decided that major public buildings should, if possible, go to architectural competition; it was quite common to have 20 to 30 competitions running at the same time. By 1975 local politicians had begun to notice that, whilst they had well-built new buildings, few were of international status. So they started inviting foreign architects to enter their competitions .

Our design for Dusseldorf displayed both 'Abstract' and 'Representational' characteristics. An entrance pavilion was, as it were, pulled out from a circular void to symbolise and represent the whole museum, which, to lessen the impact of a new building in the historic centre, was otherwise buried within the city block. The Dusseldorf project was the real beginning of our foreign involvement, and it came at a fortunate time, when we were short of work and the economic decline in England was such that from then on, there was only going to be a limited amount of prestige work. It allowed me to escape from the claustrophobic and defensive architectural climate in England, a situation which has recently become even worse.

Aspects of the programme for Dusseldorf were quite similar to those for Stuttgart: both had a central location in the city and the need to preserve existing buildings; both asked for public footpaths to cross the building site.

Our design for the Wallraf Richartz museum at Cologne, also from 1975, was likewise an invited competition which we did not win. The presence of the Cathedral may have had an overwhelming effect on our proposal. The Museum was in three parts: a long gallery wing, an intermediary entrance building and an auditorium building. The character of the new plaza was determined by a collection of architectural elements including a 'lean-to' entrance hall, a sloping exit ramp descending on the axis of a sunken sculpture court and inclined tubes of free-spanning escalators rising to the auditorium.

Staatsgalerie, Stuttgart

Our third German competition was for Stuttgart in 1977, which we did win.

On the urban level our concern was that as many of the existing buildings as possible should be retained, preserving the street character of the area. Stuttgart was bombed-out during the war and further destroyed by post-war reconstruction; preservation of what was left formed an important aspect of the competition. Where our buildings meet the street, they adopt similar scale and materials as the adjoining buildings.

The old gallery of 1837 is neo-classical and U-shaped in plan. There is a semi-circular entrance drive and at the mid point of the forecourt used to stand a classical urn, replaced in the 19th Century by an equestrian statue. The new building is also U-shaped, but instead of a semicircular drive there is a circular court. The man on a horse is reiterated by a new taxi drop-off pavilion. Mandatory in the competition was the requirement for a public footpath to cut across the site, a democratic request in many Germany competitions.

We hope the Staatsgalerie is monumental, because that is the tradition for public buildings, particularly museums. We also hope that it is informal and populist - hence the anti-monumentalism of the meandering footpath, the voided centre, the colouring and much else.

On the architectural level we were concerned that the building should evoke an 'association' of *museum*. Although it combines traditional elements with new, the traditional elements are used in a modern way, such as the 'histrionic' cornice that is used to define the sculpture terraces, or the larger and smaller assemblages of 'constructivist' canopies indicating a hierarchy of entrances.

19th-century museums have qualities I find attractive, for instance the enfilades of gallery rooms. Even when small, 19th-century museums have a certain monumentalism, although for me this has nothing to do with size or style, but rests entirely on 'presence'.

It is, of course, no longer acceptable to 'do' Classicism straight. Here the central pantheon, instead of being the culminating room, is but a void, a room-like non-space. Instead of having a dome, it is open to the sky. The plan is axial but frequently compromised; contained rooms conjoin with a 'free plan' and the public footpath meanders either side of a central axis. The casually monumental is thus diminished by the deliberately informal. The ambivalence of the 'front' corresponds to the ambiguity of the street, since Konrad Adenauer Strasse is more an autobahn than a street. Instead of a 'façade', the front recedes, presenting a collection of architectural incidents adjacent to the walking movement, into, through and over the building.

Other details which contribute to the 'monumentally informal' are the juxtaposition of stone and stucco walls with coloured metal assemblies (such as the entrance canopies); the fat tube handrails, and the 'S' curving entrance hall window; the taxi drop-off pavilion and the air intake funnels. These colourful elements help counteract the perhaps overwhelming appearance of a monumental stone quarry. Internally, green rubber flooring, an alternative to the highly polished stone more normal in Germany, reminds us that museums today are places of popular entertainment.

Also contributing to the 'monumentally informal' are the brightly coloured elevator, the sunburst ceiling lights and the curved counters. The ceiling lighting in the Kunsthalle is like that of a shopping mall, reminding us that today there is a commercial side to art and exhibitions.

The new gallery is a big success, having had almost a million visitors in the first seven months. It went from 56th place to first in the attendance ranking of German museums. As a consequence we have been asked to complete the other half of the square on Eugenstrasse and have been commissioned to design the new building for the Music and Theatre Academy.

The Architectural Review published an essay by Emilio Ambasz, who saw beyond the witticisms to the responsibilities of the new building:

> In this courtyard dwell together the spirits of Biedermeier and Schinkel. If ever a present day culture were to declare that its longings have found permanent embodiment, Germany would have to point to this courtyard. It is a reformulation of the recurring archetype of the Pantheon, but with a roof made of transient clouds. By providing a monumental frame for ineffable rituals, this courtyard stands as a metaphor for the spirit of the building, and in so doing, raises it to the exalted level of memorable architecture.

Sackler Museum, Harvard

The Sackler Museum at Harvard, an extension to the Fogg Museum in Harvard which houses the Far Eastern Collection, forms part of a series of L-shaped buildings. The following are extracts from a discussion I had with Michael Dennis, a Faculty member of Harvard's Architecture School:

> The grand stair is historically a feature in a continuous circulation sequence. But I prefer to think of this staircase as an event in itself, more a picturesque and less a sequential element in the spatial whole. I hope visitors will experience circulation through the building as a succession of minor shocks or jolts; movement through the building tends to be interrupted by stop effects and contra axes. Firstly, you go *down* instead of *up* to enter the building, then entering through the glass lobby the cross axis of the entrance hall creates a first stop movement; on the other side of the hall the long stair reverts to the axis on which you entered. Then, when the gallery at the top is reached, the axis is again at right angles, and so on. Transitional features in baroque ensembles, such as vestibules and lobbies, are here excluded, making for abrupt juxtaposition of rooms and spaces.

The galleries are intended to have the ambience of a private collection, particularly when installed in that idiosyncratic manner I associate with the Fogg.

Some observers have a problem relating the entrance façade with the side elevations because they look so different. We placed staff and tutorial rooms on the exterior with the effect of de-monumentalising that façade, producing an almost residential appearance to the street. However, no two rooms were of similar size: Harvard's planning office had produced a programme unique in that respect, and we acknowledged this complexity in the seemingly random positioning of windows, counterbalancing the effect with completely different aspects on the entrance façade.

Pressed as to what that façade represents, I would say that there is a big cleft or opening, an entrance which can also be seen as a head with a face, a visage overlooking the campus. Maybe it has a slightly Eastern and antique gaze, ambiguous as to its origin. It is not exactly a Western face; perhaps I was trying to make a face which was, shall I say, not British.

The Clore Gallery
The extension of the Tate Gallery in London, built to house the Turner Collection, is another L-shaped building. An interview with Charles Jencks was published in the opening catalogue, of which the following are extracts:

The new wing is also a garden wall containing the gardens of the Tate, and you approach by walking through these gardens. We wanted to make an entrance which did not compete with the Tate, where you go up a grand flight of steps and through a central portico. So, we turned our entrance side-on to the Tate, in deference to the established entrance. Instead of being monumental, ours is scaled down like the orangery extension to a country house.

The galleries in the new building are at the same floor level as those in the Tate. The public move from one to the other without awareness of change. We followed the same principle at Stuttgart and at the Sackler. In this case the entrance hall, auditorium, reading room etc were sunk below ground level. We then made a sunken forecourt as a transition or doorstep to the new building, so that, instead of going up monumental steps you go down into a paved garden.

The new building relates to the Tate, reversing what happens on the corner of the Tate, where a pediment sits above a lunette window. Across the forecourt, a conversation is maintained between the old and new buildings.

The stone Tate is on one side of our building and the brick Lodge on the other. Our facade tries to mediate between the two, introducing a third element, the panelled stucco. This combination allows us to soften and weld the transitions between the Tate and the Lodge.

However, the panelled stucco and Portland stone disappear when you get to the service elevation at the back making a distinction between public façades and functional elevations.

The Clore is not made of solid stone or structural brickwork like the Tate and the Lodge. Its materials are all veneers (as is the case with most modern buildings). We have tried to indicate that these veneered surfaces are not structural, hence the scissoring of walls in strategic places. When using traditional materials in an untraditional way it should be explicit that they are applied; here there's a kind of abstract slashing and cutting which can only mean these materials (and symbols) are not as substantial as they appear.

In order to exploit the walk through the entrance hall as a prelude to entering the galleries visitors come in on a zig-zag route, backwards and forwards across a central axis. First you are deflected left to the information desk, then right to go up the stairs; then you make a left back along the balcony towards the galleries and a joggle brings you in behind the arched window, back onto the cross axis of the hall. This should make an interesting entrance sequence, or show how to maximise the event within a small space. At one point the public are travelling in the opposite direction of the galleries. At the top of the stairs, they are signalled by the large arched opening to return along the balcony to enter the galleries through the arch - except that you don't go through it, you side step in behind it. The arched opening is a message, but it's not used in quite the normal way.

In the galleries there is a neutral wall zone for paintings. At the top of this is a non-functional picture rail, a division between picture wall and the angled ceiling; above this is a light scoop down which daylight is bounced onto the picture wall. The centre of the rooms is slightly darker than the walls and this should be a good atmosphere for looking at pictures.

The Bay Window is where visitors can view the gardens and the river. We would have liked more of these windows but were compromised by what the curators would accept. The form of the bays is sharp-prowed or pointed; it is as if, with some difficulty, the interior has penetrated to the exterior.

Another series of three buildings was related to the theme of 'the loggia'. This includes the plan for the library at Latina, the Berlin Science Centre and the Performing Arts Centre at Cornell University.

We were asked to design a public library in the City of Latina. Built by Mussolini, it was then called Littoria and sited on the Pontine marshes which Mussolini canaled extensively and effectively drained in the 1930s.

We placed the library across the wide end of the triangular site in the centre of town. It was to be bold and simple in contrast with the assortment of adjoining buildings, but monumental to indicate the library's civic importance. The requirement for a public park suggested the relationship of a palazzo to its garden. It was important to us as a foreground to the new building.

The loggia linking with adjoining streets overlooked the garden and would, we hoped, be used as a traditional colonnade for public promenade.

The surface of both the walls and roofs was to be in alternating courses of travertine and sandstone (similar to the Staatsgalerie). The loggia roof, its trusses and supporting columns were to be metallic - highly coloured and reflective. Unfortunately this scheme may not be built - there was a change in local government and our Client, the Mayor of the City, went out of office.

The Wissenschaftszentrum (Science Centre), Berlin
This building is really a Think Tank, a government institute for deep thinking on matters of environment, sociology and management. The old Beaux-Arts building on the site, (by the architect who built the Reichstag), somehow survived the war and had to be preserved; we have converted it for conference facilities.

In the entrance hall we removed the fountain and made an opening with steps leading down to a newly formed colonnade in the back of the old building. The visitor thus walks directly through the old building into the garden which constrains separate entrances to the new buildings.

The main requirement was for over 300 cellular office rooms (closed rooms), and we were concerned to find an architectural

9

solution for a programme almost entirely made up of repetitive small rooms.

We used the three departments – of environment, sociology and management – the element for future expansion and the library/archive (in the tower), to create a grouping of five buildings, juggled together with the old building. Within this ensemble each department has its own identifying building.

It is perhaps ironic that whilst we greatly varied the building forms, the windows were applied like wallpaper. Every room has a centrally positioned window framed with projecting architraves giving the illusion of a thick external wall and a secure (cosy) feeling inside the room.

The old and new buildings cluster around the garden, and glass roofed loggias are incorporated into the new buildings. Colonnades are formed within the old building; in all there are four arcades around the garden. We hoped to make a friendly unbureaucratic atmosphere, the opposite of an 'institutional' environment.

The primary wall surface is stucco, with each floor of alternating colour. Berlin is full of stuccoed buildings which are usually grey – dark grey – dirty grey; but they need not be grey – stucco can be any colour. Maybe I was influenced by the neo-classical buildings of Helsinki and St Petersburg which were ice blues and turquoise greens, or by buildings in Italy that are rust, burnt amber and almost orange.

The triangular loggia columns are precast concrete, supporting the gutters and trusses. Rainwater pipes travel down the centre of columns which are separately tuned like organ pipes to make a musical sound when a heavy downpour of rain flows through them. When the weather is really depressing, a metaphysical sound, a bit like Japanese music, should be heard coming from the loggias.

The following is taken from a speech made on the occasion of the opening day:

One of the good things we have found in Germany is the high quality of modern craftsmanship we have experienced both with the Staatsgalerie and also here, although I'm told that what you see is not always quite as we drew it.

This reminds me of an early experience I had with Palladio's villas. When I was a young architect I admired his buildings but only knew them from photographs. I imagined them to be made of the finest marbles. It was only later when visiting them that I discovered that the beautiful columns were in fact made of stucco on brick or sometimes just stucco on rubble.

It's a memorable day for everyone who has been involved in this project. We are adding a colourful new animal - perhaps a zebra - to the distinguished architectural zoo of Berlin's 'cultural forum'.

Now that our building is finished, I'm sure that some critical comments will have to be revised. I have in mind those critics who likened it to a collection of historic buildings. We always knew that in three dimensions it would appear quite differently: more a panorama of informal continuous buildings around a space, not a classical space, but one more akin to a college garden.

Of course, we would like to see the upper floors added to the building above the cafeteria. Meanwhile we have to be content with this fragment which reminds me of that incomplete single-storey palazzo in Venice which houses the Peggy Guggenheim collection, although ours is more a folly in a garden than a folly on a canal (it might have become so if Hans Hollein had been able to pursue his idea of flooding the back of our site).

I hope those who come to live here will find time to leave their rooms and stroll around the gardens and through the buildings, finding a place for contemplation, a contrast with the evermore efficiently computerised reality of the working day.

I am told the building appears to some as a wedding cake, so on this happy occasion I would thank all of you who have come to the celebration

The Performing Arts Center, Cornell University

Situated in up-state New York, the centre is on the edge of Cascadilla Gorge just off the campus facing over a deep gorge towards the University. Prominently sited on College Avenue, it adjoins the bridge over the Gorge, reinforcing that entrance to the campus and strengthening the link between town and gown. We planned a group of buildings connected by a 'loggia', appropriate for the picturesque nature of the Gorge. Entry is via the loggia, a promenade approach with spectacular views towards the campus and Lake Cayuga beyond. The entrance foyer at the centre of the loggia connects the major spaces, encouraging student/faculty interaction between theatre, dance and film groups, bringing them into contact with the public when there is a performance. The foyer opens onto the loggia allowing audiences to stroll in and out and take the in view in the intermissions.

The following extract is from the speech I made at the opening day:

It's a pleasure to be here in our completed building now that it is occupied and functioning. I am asked to give lectures on our work in architecture schools all over the world, and on a few occasions I have found myself in a theatre. The first time I had to perform on stage was at the Teatro de la Feniche in Venice where the University has thousands of architectural students; it was the biggest room available and I felt as if I was in a Marx Brothers movie. Maybe that experience influenced the shape of the room we are now in.

I hope that all our buildings are unique and that this one may be especially unique as it has a front side and a side side and two back sides, - most of our buildings have a back side but two back sides is unusual. I could say that there was never enough finance for this ambitious project - but perhaps that is unfair, as we chose to overspend on the two main façades and correspondingly under-spent on the other two.

I hope someday soon a Mozart opera will be performed in the Proscenium Theatre (there is an orchestra pit), and a three-ring circus will be held in the Flexible Theatre; a topless gogo dancer will appear in the bay window of the dance studio. Grand Kabuki will be staged in the loggia and there will be street performers in the plaza.

One of my last site visits coincided with the University's 'Open Day' when parents come with their sons and daughters to view the academic scene before committing their offspring. I sat outside the café across College Avenue and a family group came by; they stopped and stared at the building long and hard. Finally I heard one of them say, 'Well, I guess it's some sort of Florentine rip off' which I took to be a compliment. So I hope all who come to learn and teach in this Italianate hill village will enjoy the experience.

Compton Verney Opera House

We here reduced the apparent height of the stagehouse by the forward positioning of an entrance loggia and restaurant bridge. Viewed from the mansion house across the lake, the stagehouse and auditorium will recede in perspective behind the foreground of loggia and restaurant bridge. An entrance loggia allows visitors to approach from several directions, forming a backdrop to the new lawn. The entrance hall is triangular in plan with cloakrooms and bookshop to the right and box office and auditorium to the left. The administration pavilion encloses a garden court with public facilities at ground level.

The restaurant, which is in fact three restaurants, bridges the lake and a public footway along the edge of the bridge connects the loggia with a new garden amphitheatre. This allows a variety of public walks around the lake and places to picnic on champagne and cold salmon during the long interval. The fan-shaped restaurants have fine westerly views over the landscape, the lake and the mansion house.

In good weather, passengers would disembark at the gatehouse and walk from there through the gardens to the Opera House. The curved Sequoia avenue forms a grand approach, drawing visitors towards the lawn and entrance loggia. Walking down the avenue, views of the obelisk, the Adam bridge, the lake and the mansion house would gradually come into view in sequence. In bad weather (and if visitors are handicapped) vehicles would be directed to the drop-off circle at the end of the loggia and from there visitors could walk into the Opera House under cover.

We intended to bring the Vanbrughian mansion house, the Adam bridge, the new Opera House and the garden amphitheatre into a *jardin anglais* (both formal and informal), a dialogue between past and present across the lake. The buildings and garden elements are arranged as pavilions and follies around the end of the lake and the perceptive visitor should discover the picturesque relationships between landscape and buildings.

The Science Library, University of Irvine, Southern California
To enhance the developing bio-science mall, we suggested to the University that the new library be located *astride* its axis, spanning over the public route like a gatehouse. Thus the building will be highly visible, approached from the existing inner circle and from the bio-science quadrangle in the opposite direction. The gateway enlivens the existing plaza on the inner circle and makes a portal for the future bio-science quadrangle. The design is specific to the tradition of the Irvine Campus with its masterplan of several 'spoke' malls radiating from the original hub of the Campus. The promenade and courtyard provide a spatial sequence for visitors entering or leaving the library, and for those passing under the building and down the bio-science mall.

An entrance colonnade is the first in a sequence of contracting and expanding spaces. Splayed walls focus towards the court indicating entry and passage through the building. The central courtyard allows the entrance to be at the heart of the building and the open court provides daylight to the interior. The circular form focuses the composition and allows the building to face in both directions – a narrow gateway to the wall, where it fits between existing buildings, and a wide expansive façade that will flank the yet to be developed bio-sciences quadrangle.

The new building is unlike a civic library in a town where there is a single grand reading. Instead a variety of reader spaces and stack areas are distributed throughout the building. Readers are close to windows, seated with small groups of colleagues, not in a vast array of reading tables. Visitors enter through an entrance/exhibition hall. A fancy staircase and three elevators rise to the second level where the interlibrary loans and reserve desk is situated. Reference books and periodicals are stored together in a double height room which encircles the lower part of the court. This layout allows for flexibility; users may move from one section to another around the complete circle. Reading and bookstack areas on the fourth, fifth and sixth floors occupy the centre of the building. Each has three stack zones at right angles to the court, which becomes triangular at the upper levels, and again there is all round circulation without dead ends. Groups of study carrels line the outer wall and areas between

stacks have reading tables with views into the court.

Administration and Public Services are in the long wing. Small reading rooms and study rooms terminate these wings; they are double height and overlook the new quadrangle. The short wings have reading areas overlooking the entrance plaza. Education resources are at ground level with a separate entrance in the courtyard opposite the library entrance.

There are approx 7,000 linear feet of book stacks and spaces for over 2,000 readers. The exterior is surfaced in stone and stucco with overhanging roof eaves which conceal service plants on the roof. Construction will be completed in 1992.

Palazzo Citterio, Milan, The Extension to the Brera Museum
The Palazzo Citterio was built as an 18th-century Milanese patrician residence, in the 'Barocchetto' style. During the 200 years of its life Palazzo Citterio has seen many transformations in taste and use: from Barocchetto to Neo-Classical and Neo-gothic; from the Novecento, to the post-war period. By 1970, when the building came into the hands of the Brera, both interior and exterior were a 'mish-mash' of successive superimposed interventions.

In 1986, we were appointed by the *Friends of the Brera* to re-organise it as a museum of international stature, with emphasis on temporary and travelling exhibitions, and display of twentieth-century Italian art. The programme also required the ususal facilities for modern museums: lecture-rooms, bookshops and a cafeteria. The garden was to be restored, allowing visitors to walk through from the Palazzo Citterio to the Palazzo Brera, interconnecting the two museums.

Our Intervention (an Italian word) consisted of amalgamating the historic remains of the Palace with a series of new 'pieces' inserted where the building had already been extensively modified. The most important are:

1 A new building to contain a library, archives and a cafeteria. The volume and footprint of this new wing was determined by an earlier neo-classical addition that was demolished after 1970.
2 A new public stair, which we placed on the long axis of the courtyard. This provides direct access to a large exhibition room in the basement.
3 A new core of lifts and stairs positioned on the cross-axis of the courtyard, a point of departure and return for circuits of exhibitions at piano nobile and second floor level, as well as an access to the exhibition galleries at ground and first floor level and to the lecture and seminar rooms in the basement.
4 A new roof with a glazed cupola covering the courtyard; this makes a visual separation between the lower levels of courtyard facades, (which are original), and the upper levels (which are a recent addition). This cupola/roof enables the courtyard to function as the entrance hall, accessible to all parts of the museum.
5 A new open courtyard flanked by the rear façade of the palazzo and by the new library wing, a staircase and bridge which begin the high-level connection to Palazzo Brera.
6 A new open-air amphitheatre through which the public can rise into the garden enroute from the basement exhibition gallery.

These interventions will reinstate the palace and its gardens and enrich the entry from Via Brera into the covered courtyard, the sequence being through the open courtyard and amphitheatre, to the remains of the *giardino all' inglese* (complete with artificial romantic grotto) which will be repaired.

The street façade of Palazzo Citterio is articulated in three bays with two entrance archways. The principal archway leads into the covered courtyard; the second allows independent public access to the ground level exhibition hall. The covered courtyard will be the focus of public arrival, meetings, and access to galleries. Existing openings are re-utilised and lead to greater or lesser functions according to their degree of monumentality. The courtyard floor, contrasting bands of coloured cobbles in an octagonal pattern, is typically Milanese and will be preserved. New elements include a large counter for information and ticket sales and a seating bench around the column which supports the cupola.

The cafeteria is planned as a typical Milanese bar with some small tables for those who prefer to sit and a long counter serving drinks and snacks. The front wall is a glazed screen which in the mild season can be opened to spread tables and sunshades into the courtyard.

First Basement
The new stair descending from the entrance court arrives in a vaulted space from which a ramp leads back to the basement lecture theatre and seminar rooms. There is a wide balcony from which a double stair descends into the temporary exhibition hall, which in turn has external doors allowing public access to the amphitheatre and garden. The basement lecture theatre and seminar rooms can be reached via the alternative entrance in the evenings and at times when the museum is closed.

Piano Nobile
The stairs and lifts ascend to a wide landing with windows overlooking the entrance court. From here the public can visit the exhibition rooms or donations rooms which are *ensuite*, behind the front and rear façades of the palace.

Second Floor
The second floor area will be subdivided into exhibition rooms arranged in a circuit echoing the plan at first floor level. On the garden façade is a sitting room where visitors have a view of the garden. The archive and library area in the new wing can be reached from the entrance hall. It will be used by art historians, librarians and scholars. The library has a top-lit double-height reading room and mezzanine. A bay window overlooks the garden and a balcony allows outside reading in good weather. Construction of these works will probably begin shortly.

Residential Park at Canary Wharf, London Docks
We proposed a large riverside park with terraces stepping down to the Thames. Semi-enclosed on the island side, with linear buildings containing offices, shops and a hotel, apartment towers are ranged informally along the river front. The Parks surround the existing West Ferry Road Circus, a large multi-level roundabout. The approach roads and circus will be incised into stepped terraces. The roundabout is under construction, included in our design unchanged, other than being crowned by a garden maze.

The airy spaciousness of the Park will give an arcadian contrast to the 'downtown' commercial area of Canary Wharf, which has been built by Americans with a US image. The park has public open space accessible to residents, office workers and adjoining communities. It would form an interesting 'foreground' to downtown Canary Wharf. The varied building forms and reflective surfaces should create a dramatic river-edge. The stepped terraces are surfaced alternately with gravel and grass and are connected by short ramps. They have stone retaining walls, trees and planting.

The River also contributes to the environmental experience and an esplanade is proposed, a public promenade for evening and weekend strolling, connecting Limehouse with the Isle of Dogs. A loggia with pubs, restaurants and shopping provides covered access to the offices. A riverbus pier extends into the river and the loggia provides a protected route for river commuters.

The hotel is in a diagonal building on the eastern edge; a cinema complex below the north east corner of the Park is entered through a pyramidal advertising pavilion.

The apartment towers would have views of the Thames, the City, West India Dock and Canary Wharf. Each tower has an approach road to an entrance lobby and car ramps lead to parking garages below.

The residential area is designed as a series of mini towers, radically different from the solid mass of the first project, yet yielding the same number of apartments. The towers are stepped by virtue of three different floor plans which provide a variety of apartment types. The terrace steps could adjoin the Restaurant and Health Club/Gymnasium facilities, which, in fine weather, would open onto the roofs, wind protected by high glazed screens.

Los Angeles Philharmonic Hall
We hope to achieve an identity for the new concert halls (known as the Disney Centre) by combining the tradition of monumental civic buildings with the populist aspect of today's places of culture and entertainment.

Our design is an ensemble of architectural forms corresponding to the functional elements of the programme. They are unified at ground level with a public concourse, the microcosm of a city. The concert hall which holds two and a half thousand people is the centre-piece; its diagonal orientation to the corner reinforces Grand Avenue as *the* boulevard for the whole of the music centre - existing and proposed. The concert hall (named Snowflake), the chamber hall (named Shoe Box) and the support facilities building (named the Villa) form a trio of elements.

A smaller group of three pavilions contain the shop, the cinema and the club. They indicate entrances and are a visual foil to the large single form of the existing Chandler building. A circular electronic billboard above the shop announces current events at the Disney Centre.

The garden is enclosed on three sides by the support facility building (the Villa), which opens towards downtown L A. The upper parts of building partly enclose roof terraces with adjoining bars and lounges that offer views of Los Angeles and the Hollywood hills.

The concourse is transparent, highly visible and accessible. It involves the surrounding streets, inviting entry from all sides. Like the concourse of Grand Central in New York, it can be approached from several directions.

The complex incorporates lobbies, galleries, meeting areas, bars and lounges, free-planned to encourage sightseeing. Floor level changes articulate activities and provide over-looks for people-watching. An illuminated floor beneath the crystalline soffit of the concert hall is flanked by elevator towers defining the centre, which is animated by flying escalators guiding audiences to the ringways around the concert hall.

By closing vertical access to the halls, public movement through the concourse would be allowed during the day. Flooded by natural light from all sides, it should make a friendly place to meet, purchase tickets and gifts, listen to recitals or lectures, see exhibitions and visit the garden - a bustling centre encouraging visitors and tourists to explore the world of music. In the evening the concourse would be ablaze with light, like a beacon or magic lantern.

The concert hall (Snowflake) has tiered seating balconies clustering around the stage, placing the conductor and orchestra almost in the centre of the room, unifying the audience and orchestra with the intensified impact of a live performance. The balconies seat from 70 to 150, so the individual is never lost in a large mass of people (a more regular version of Scharoun's Berlin Philharmonie).

The Chamber Hall (Shoe-box) is on a traditional plan for small ensembles, recitalists and soloists, with 800 seats on a level floor and 300 on a balcony around three sides of the room.

A cinema has been included for movies and public lectures. Using live circuit relay it could function as overspill for concerts.

The Villa houses the musicians, performers and administration activities. Rooms are arranged to encourage an in-house community.

Tokyo International Forum

Our design for the Tokyo International Forum emphasised its cultural importance by placing a tall building and a public plaza in its centre on the axis of the Imperial Palace. The VIP entrance through the plaza is on this axis.

Transparent buildings are placed on a stone base which could be considered as the traditional counterpart to the 'technological' structures above; or as a hill with approach paths to the 'City Crown'. The circular plaza which forms part of the base is enclosed by a wall of stone.

The building's organisation has been determined by functional requirements of its visitors and delegates; by the need for earthquake resistant structures (with thousands of people); and by the need for emergency evacuation arising from the very high density of occupancy. Primary volumes are articulated as separate forms connected by the base which contains the public concourse, information exchanges, galleries, restaurants, shops, etc. At the north and south ends of the building are Hall A for 5,000 and Halls B and C for 1,500 and 2,000 persons respectively. Large trade exhibition halls are placed below street level parallel to a travelator connecting Keiyo and Yurakucho subway stations.

The tower has smaller conference facilities in hexagonal, circular and semicircular volumes. The upper semicircular part contains a luxury restaurant and administrative offices; the restaurant opens to a roof terrace. At street level the public concourse is the major gathering place – a literal exchange of people and activities. Visitors from the subways below and from the adjoining streets converge in a triple-height space below the tower. Escalators and elevators rise to the delegates' concourse which in turn allows access to the large halls.

The distinction between the concourse at street level which is open to tourists and the upper delegate/ticket holder concourse for audiences is important: the upper concourse is only accessible to delegates and performance ticket holders.

Bookshop for the Venice Biennale

The Biennale site is that large public garden near the Arsenal which houses exhibition buildings from various countries set as pavilions among the trees. The largest will be the new Italian building which is to be rebuilt.

Coming from the Vaporetto or the centre of Venice, visitors approach through the trees to a semicircular paved entrance terrace. The building is flanked on one side by the access to the Italian building and on the other by a garden theatre which is used for openings and events.

Our 'bookship - boatshop' is a long low pavilion fitting between the trees. An illuminated roof sign indicates the entrance and a laser will send beams of coloured light through the overhanging branches into the sky, a marker visible from the lagoon. Overhanging eaves project over the boardwalk which runs round the three glazed sides of the bookshop. This roof creates a shaded awning over the long shop window which has a permanent display of the art books and catalogues on sale within. Books will be laid out along a continuous timber bench, and there is shelving for storage below. They will be paid for and packed at the counter near the entrance.

Metal roof trusses also support a central duct which carries air-conditioning, main lighting, alarm system etc. The plantroom is over the entrance lobby and a pair of opening ventilation shutters allows replacement of machinery from outside.

I cannot deny that there are stylistic similarities between buildings in a series, but they are worked out, perhaps exhausted after three or four variants. But it's no accident that I have mainly described our designs in factual terms. We proceed by analysis leading to logical decisions, along a linear route, trying to add one good idea/decision to another. I think every building must have at least two good ideas. But this hardly ever comes in the form of the blinding flash. This might work with a single purpose building, say an office block or a football stadium, but our projects are usually multi-functional, to say the least.

So, for me 'functionalism' remains the guiding principal, and, I hope, the basis of our concepts (which can include reference and association where it enlightens). Indeed I regard the theory of functionalism as *the* major 20th-century contribution to architectural progress.

I hope this has indicated that our work avoids the easy 'cop out' of minimalist Modernism or high-tech styling, and the self-indulgence of silly Post-Modernism. There is a more direct and thoughtful way, down an avenue of functional appropriateness which can be sought and followed.

On Prince Charles & Architecture

Q   What do you think of Prince Charles?

A   Well - he's managed to set back the cause of good modern architecture in this country by 50 years - though I know he would have liked to set it back 200 years - everything Georgian.
He seems unable to distinguish between good modern architecture and bad modern architecture - it's a problem for him and it's a problem for us.
*   I believe he's encased by a reactionary group of advisors, - historians, preservationists, and intellectuals who hate progressive modern architecture and he's not getting balanced or moderate opinion. Even so his personal addition of false columns and pediment, to Highgrove, - a decent Regency Villa, - was I think in questionable taste.*
Italy has just built 16 new football stadiums using good modern architects; Germany has built over forty new museums and galleries using good modern architects from Germany and abroad. Paris has recently built seven prestige Mitterand buildings using good modern architects. What has Britain done? - we have printed a book called 'A Vision of Britain'.

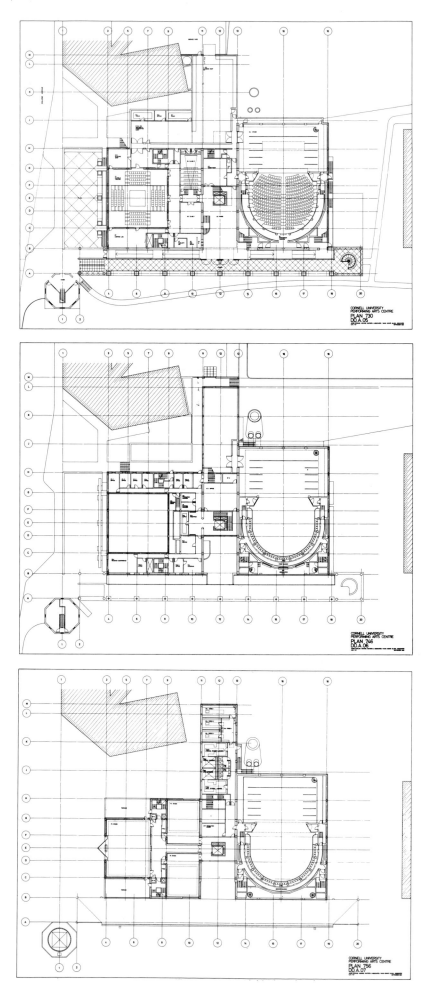

FLOOR PLANS: GROUND, FIRST & UPPER

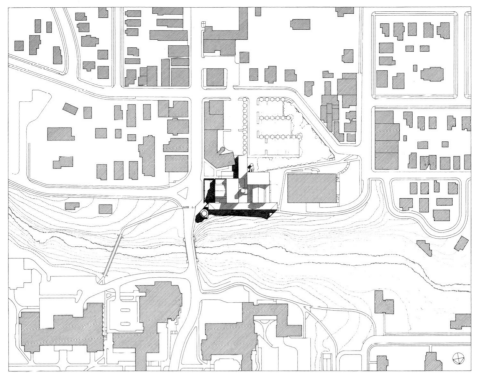

*ABOVE:*SITE PLAN; *BELOW:* MODEL PHOTOGRAPH

PERFORMING ARTS CENTER
CORNELL UNIVERSITY

The Performing Arts Centre is a teaching facility for theatre arts and a performance centre for the University. Prominently sited on College Avenue, close to the bridge over Cascadilla Gorge, the new building stands as a gateway to the campus. A cluster of theatre volumes is configured by a loggia, relating to the small town character of College Avenue and the picturesque view of the gorge. The off-campus location draws audiences from both town and gown. The three-storey entrance hall is also the main foyer for the proscenium and flexible theatres, opening on to the loggia. The elevator extends upwards like a *campanile, announcing the Centre to downtown Ithaca. Visitors can descend from the entrance foyer to the Dance Performance Studio which has multiple entrances and overviewing control booths. Costume shop areas are linked by back-stage stairs to all performance and production spaces. Additional studios and classrooms for the theatre, dance and film departments are housed in the flexible theatre block. The Scenery Shop at the rear, opens through sound-isolating doors which enable vehicles to be driven on stage. The top floor rises above surrounding roofs allowing faculty offices views in several directions.*

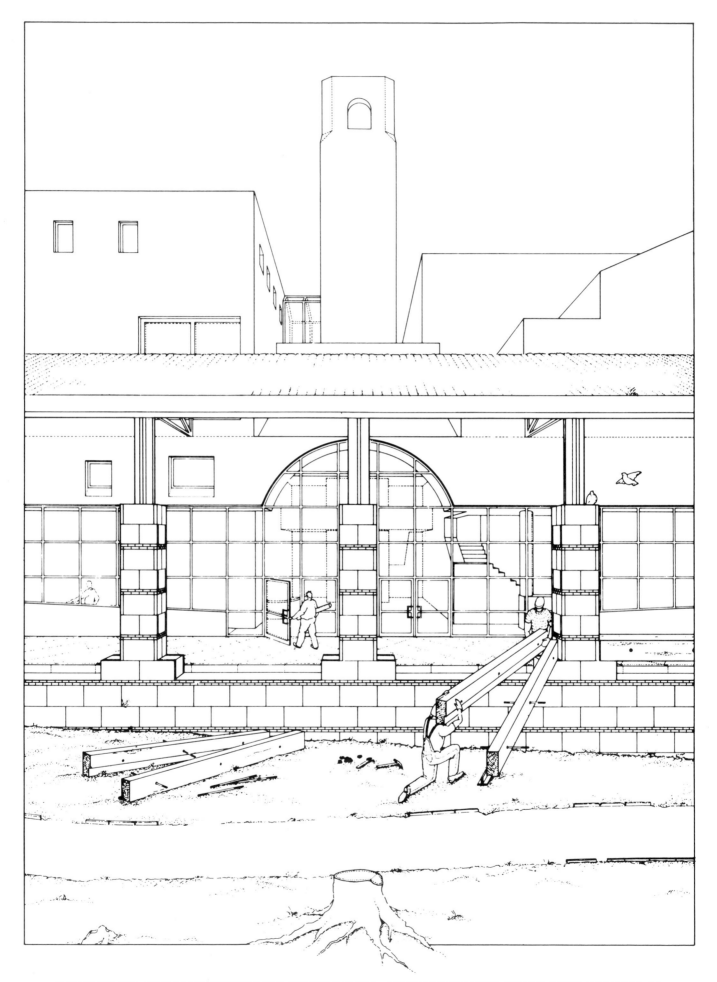

ABOVE: PERSPECTIVE CONSTRUCTION SKETCH OF LOGGIA AND ENTRANCE HALL; OPPOSITE: VIEW FROM WEST; OVERLEAF: COLLEGE AVENUE FACADE

OPPOSITE: DANCE STUDIO WINDOW THROUGH LOGGIA; *ABOVE*:OCTAGONAL PAVILION; *OVERLEAF*: COLLEGE AVENUE FACADE AT NIGHT

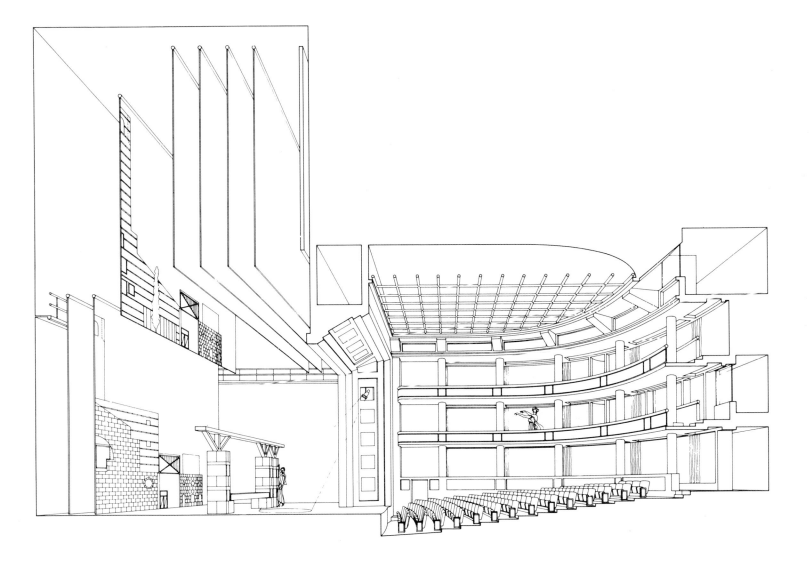

OPPOSITE: SEATING LEVELS WITHIN THE PROSCENIUM THEATRE; *ABOVE*: PERSPECTIVE SECTION THROUGH PROSCENIUM THEATRE

PERSPECTIVE SECTION THROUGH LOGGIA AND ENTRANCE HALL

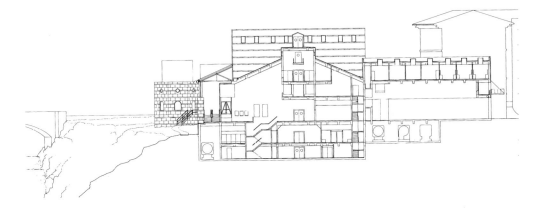

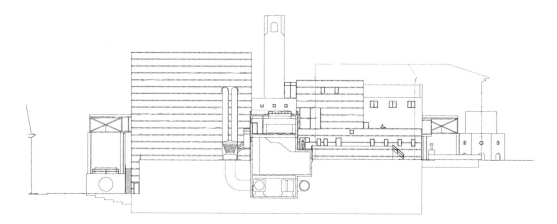

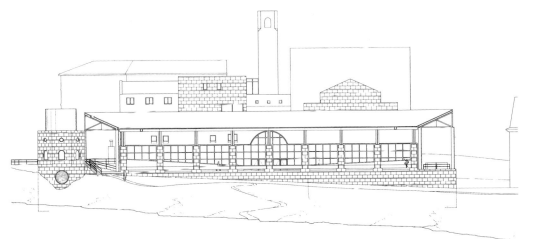

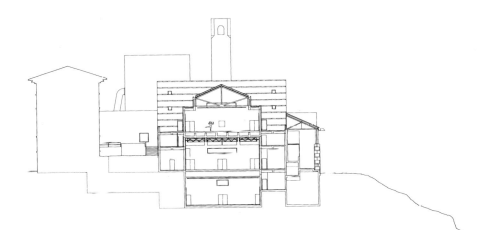

CROSS SECTIONS

27

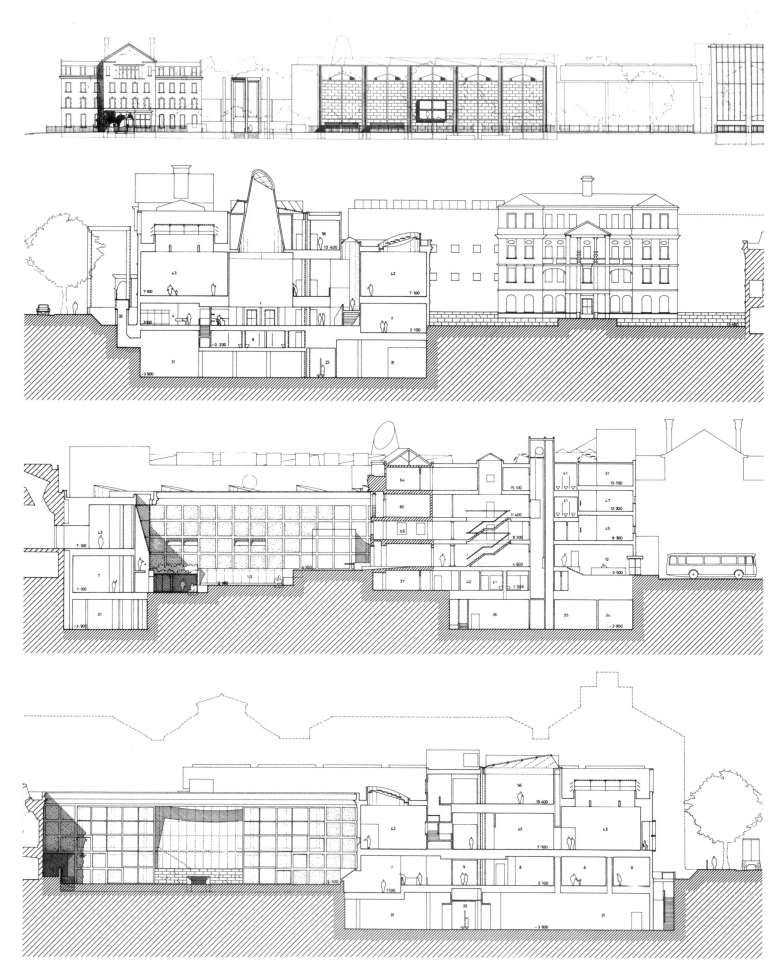

ABOVE: JOHN ISLIP STREET ELEVATION; *BELOW*: CROSS SECTIONS

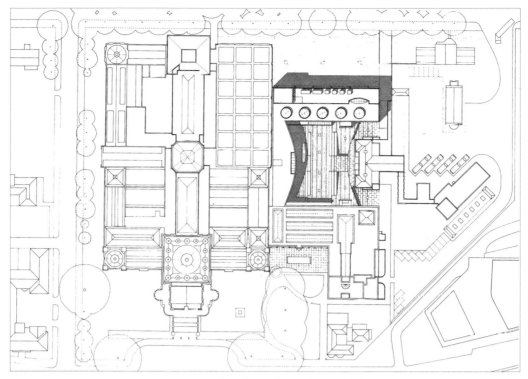

ABOVE: SITE PLAN; *BELOW*: MODEL PHOTOGRAPH

MUSEUMS OF NEW ART & SCULPTURE
TATE GALLERY, LONDON

The building of the new museums is the next stage in the Tate Gallery's development of the Queen Alexandra Hospital site. The designs include museums and a study centre, which could be constructed in one, two or three phases. An entrance hall provides access to the new museums, either side of the line of double columns delineating the areas of the first and second phase buildings. Arrival is accentuated by the bowed glass window which flexes outward, overlooking the sculpture garden. The entrance hall is connected by a curved stair with the circulation space which provides an exhibition area for use of either museum. The form of the Modern Sculpture Museum will balance with the Clore Gallery, creating an outdoor Sculpture Garden between. The New Art Museum has gallery spaces of differing character on three floors.

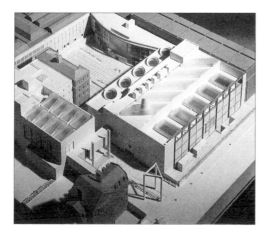

PERSPECTIVE OF STREET FACADE

ABOVE: AXONOMETRIC; *BELOW L TO R*: FLOOR PLAN, SITE PLAN, FLOOR PLAN

NUMBER 1 POULTRY, MANSION HOUSE
CITY OF LONDON

The design for Number 1 Poultry relates to existing street patterns and to Bank Junction which is surrounded by several historic buildings, for example The Bank of England by Soane, Lutyens' Midland Bank and St. Mary Woolnoth by Hawksmoor. All the historic buildings are symmetrical in plan although they face onto an informal street pattern. To relate to these historic examples, Number 1 Poultry is planned about a central axis with similar façades to Queen Victoria Street and Poultry; the parapet height corresponds to surrounding buildings. The new building contains shops, offices, roof garden and restaurant. At pavement level a pedestrian passage through the central arches links the shopping colonnades through a circular court which is open to the sky and connects with Bank Underground Station below. Daylighting through the court reaches the centre of the building at each level. Public access to the offices is from the court. The VIP entrance at the apex of the building leads to the central court above the public passage way. Lifts connect the levels of the court and all floors with the rooftop garden and restaurant. The building surfaces will be stone-veneered concrete with bronze finishes.

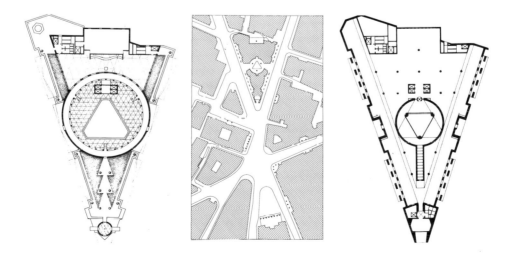

PERSPECTIVE OF PART OF MAIN GALLERY

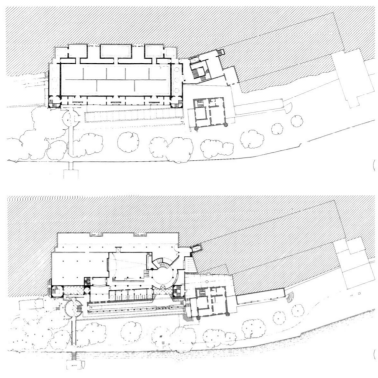

ABOVE: TOP LEVEL PLAN; *CENTRE*: ENTRANCE LEVEL PLAN; *BELOW*: MODEL PHOTOGRAPH

THYSSEN ART GALLERY
VILLA FAVORITA, LUGANO

The building is planned on three floors with a mezzanine, sited behind the old colonnade which would form a scenic approach to the entrance. It is connected to the old gallery and Villa Ghirlanda below terrace level, avoiding a high level connection which might disrupt the arcadian setting. The form of the new gallery will be on the scale of other buildings on the estate, whilst maintaining its own identity. It will appear private and 'un-museumlike' by blending with the romantic character of the villas. The exterior will be finished in stucco and terracotta as on existing buildings. The entrances to the picture galleries have protective screen walls to prevent overspill of light into the exhibition areas. These entrance screens incorporate seats where a pause from the visit can be taken. Daylighting will be through roof lanterns above laylights using diffusing glass, a development of the laylight system in the existing gallery.

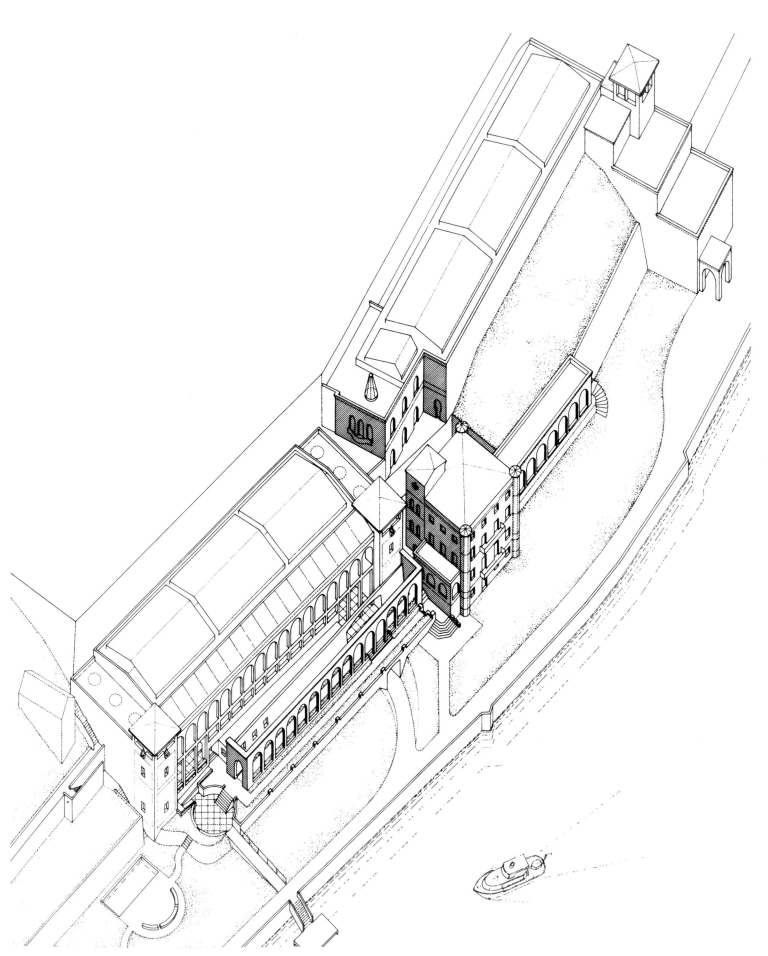

AXONOMETRIC OF THE SCHEME

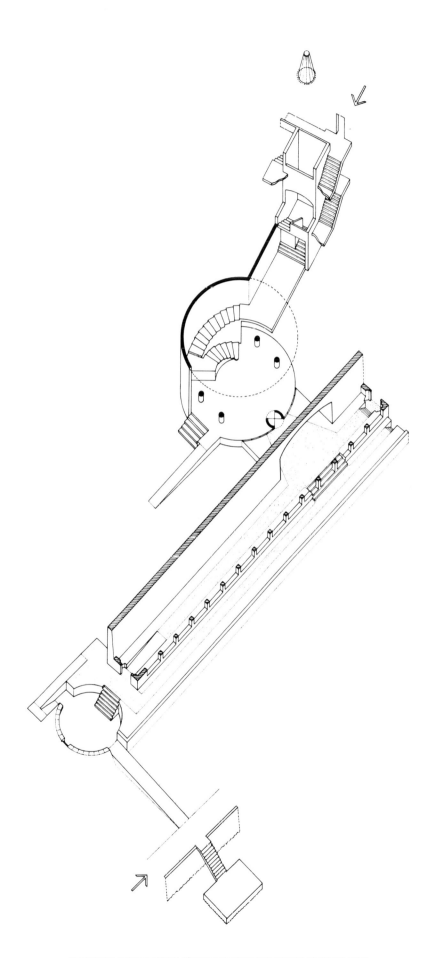

DISSECTED AXONOMETRIC OF PROMENADE THROUGH THE NEW BUILDING

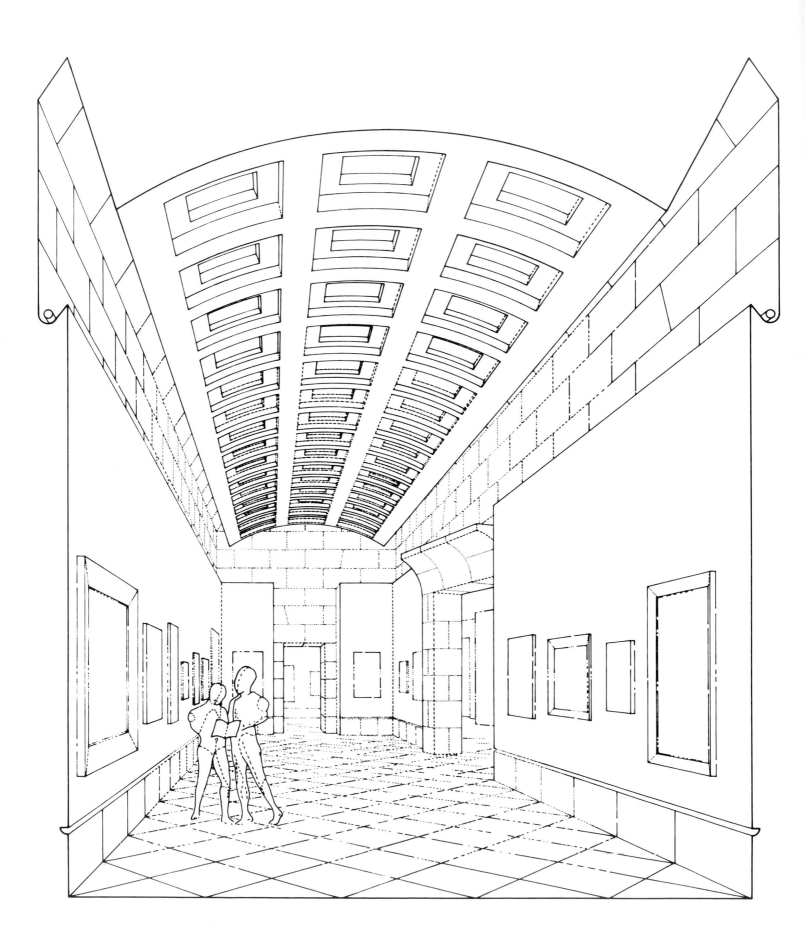

PERSPECTIVE OF SMALL SIDE GALLERY

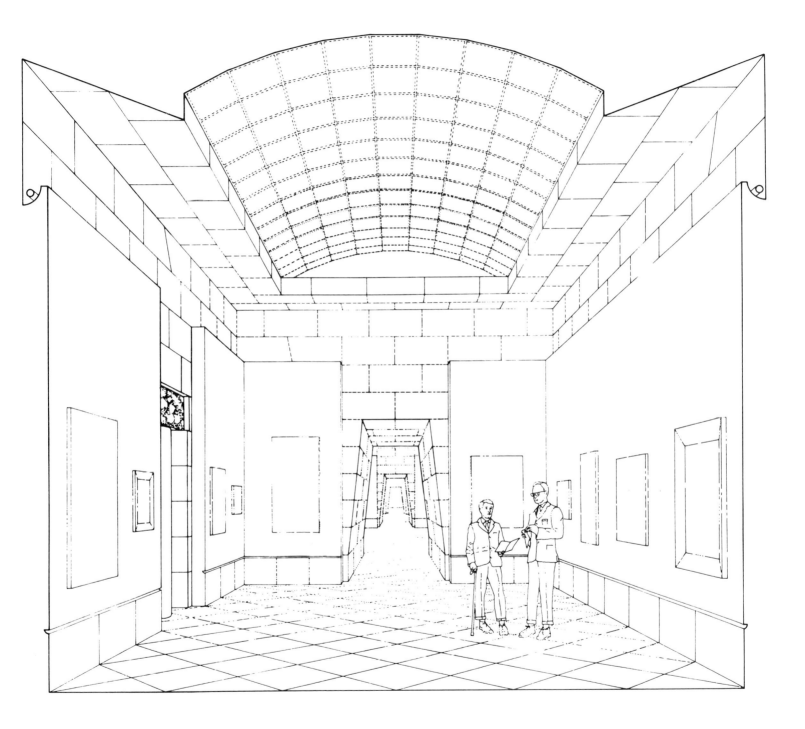

PERSPECTIVE OF SMALL SIDE GALLERY

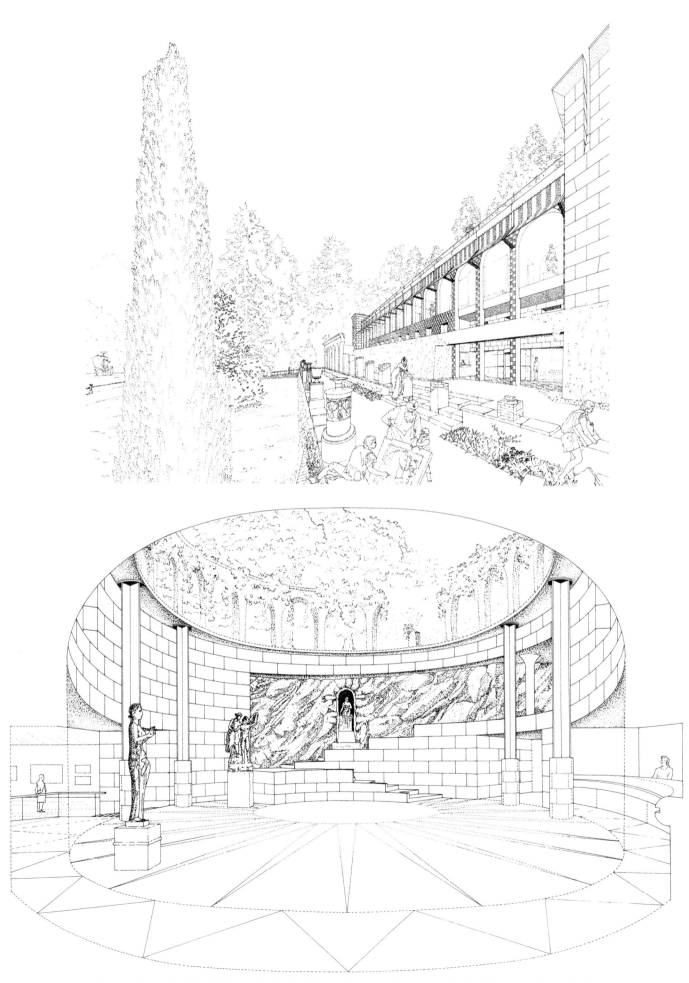

ABOVE: LAKESIDE EXTERIOR PERSPECTIVE SHOWING JUXTAPOSITION OF NEW AND OLD COLONNADE; *BELOW*: ENTRANCE HALL

ABOVE: LAKESIDE VIEW; *BELOW*: CROSS SECTION THROUGH CANTEEN AND OLD COLONNADE

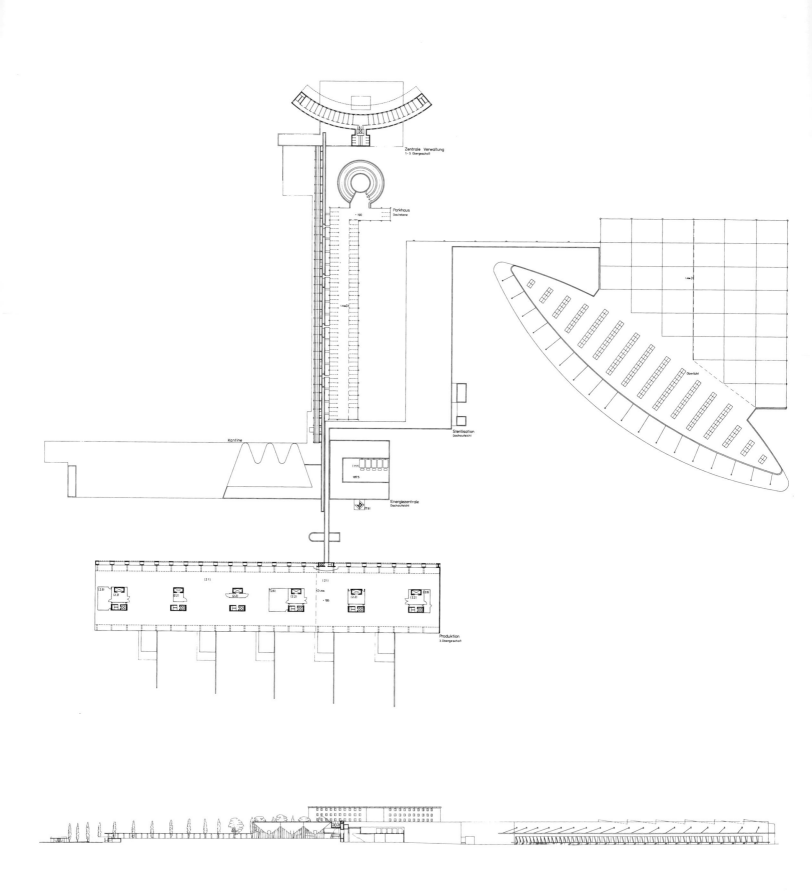

Zentrale Verwaltung
1 - 3 Obergeschoß

Parkhaus
Dachebene

Sterilisation
Dachaufsicht

Kantine

Energiezentrale
Dachaufsicht

Produktion
3.Obergeschoß

ABOVE: UPPER FLOOR PLAN; *BELOW*: SOUTH ELEVATION

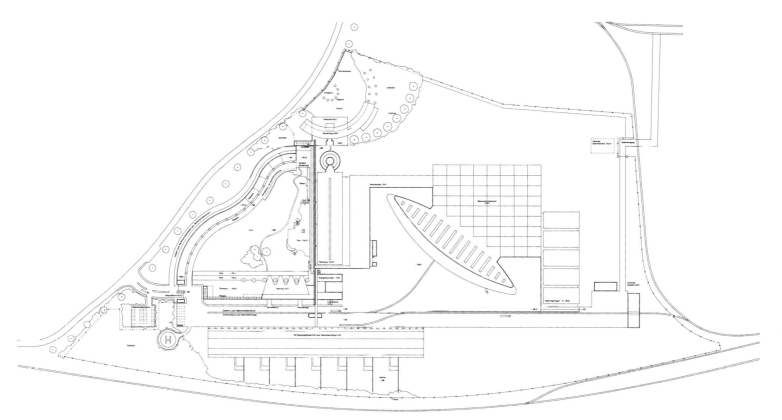

ABOVE: SITE PLAN; *BELOW*: MODEL PHOTOGRAPH

BRAUN HEADQUARTERS
MELSUNGEN, WEST GERMANY
in association with Walter Naegeli

The site for the headquarters and production buildings of a company manufacturing medical products lies within a few miles of the small North German town of Melsungen. Situated at the junction of two pretty river valleys, its size is such that the main bulk of buildings is considerably larger than the medieval centre of Melsungen. Our project proposes to add architectural features to the landscape, thus interpreting it and completing it in an architectural sense. The project also shows how factory requirements can be harmonised with the park architecture.

The programme required parking for 1,300 cars outside the security perimeter, so that employees could be checked past security counters. So we proposed a multi-storey carpark, only accessible via a bridge connecting the two highest places on the site. The front of the site is designed as a triangular park with a little river, a pond, terraces and pergolas; a stone-clad wall forms the background for the bridge, overgrown with vines and detailed like a winter garden. The back has a triangular industrial courtyard serving the surrounding buildings .

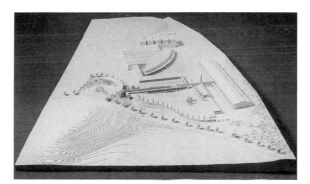

ABOVE: AXONOMETRIC OF STRUCTURAL DETAIL; *BELOW*: WEST ELEVATION

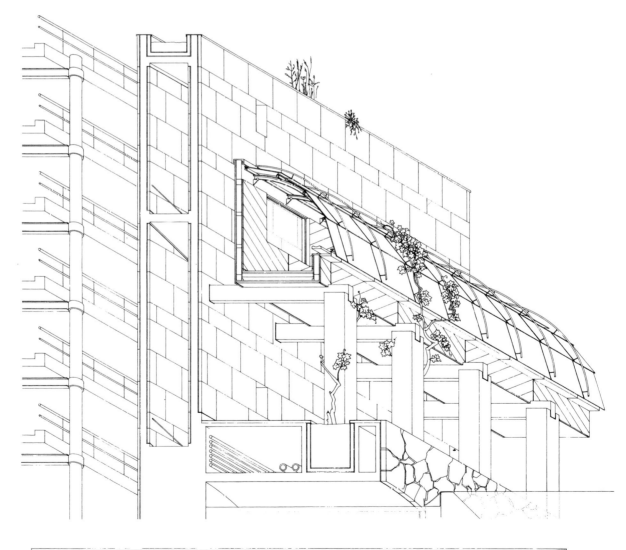

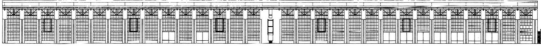

ABOVE: AXONOMETRIC OF STRUCTURAL DETAIL; *BELOW*: PARTIAL ELEVATION

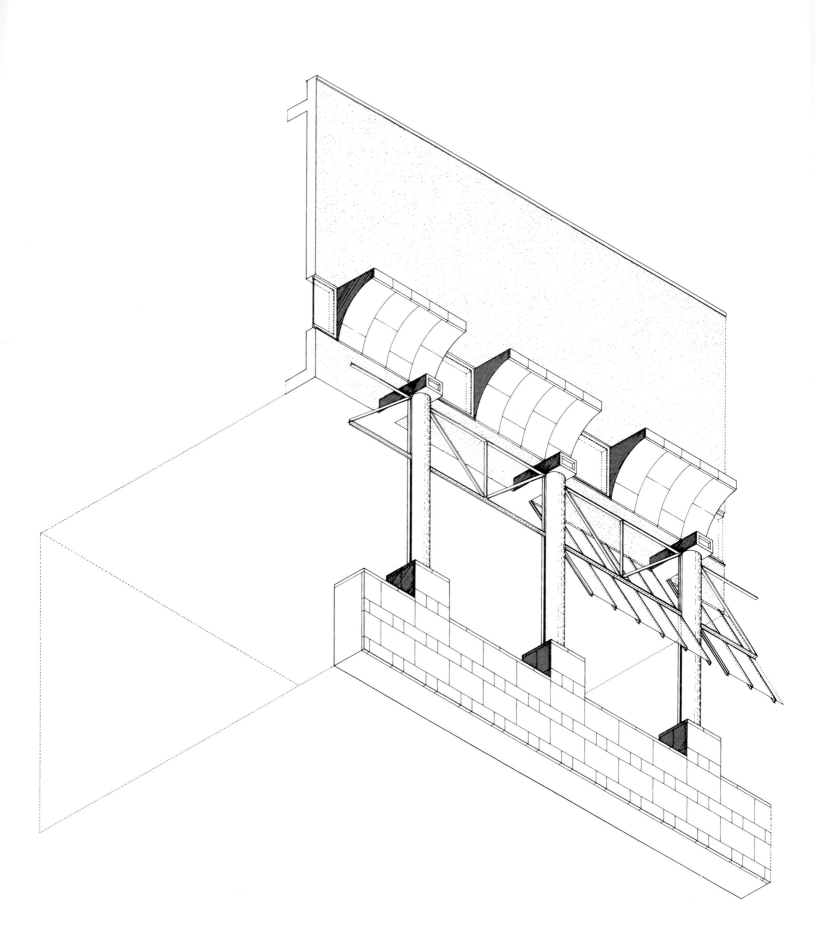

AXONOMETRIC OF STRUCTURAL DETAIL

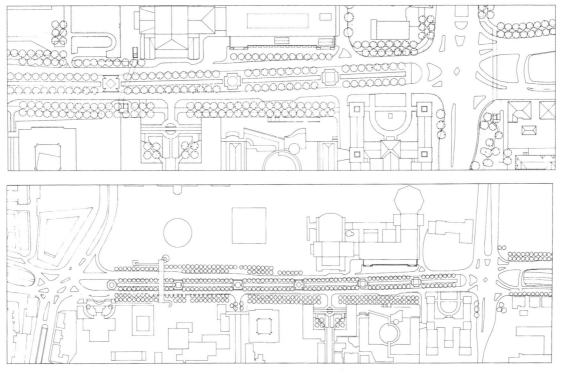

ABOVE: SITE PLANS *BELOW*: MODEL PHOTOGRAPH

STATE THEATRE WAREHOUSE
STUTTGART

The design of our façade emphasises the lower levels, reversing the emphasis given to the top by the outjutting upper storey of the existing building. Thus the building's scale is reduced, making a ground level arcade the main architectural element, screening the service access and sheltering the loading dock. The existing façade is partially included as a secondary elevation behind the arcade. Articulated end pavilions which frame the new façade have inclined surfaces for the display of banners and billboards. The new façade is 'representative', complimenting the Staatsgalerie with similar alternation of stone courses and stucco.

A dropped cornice reflects the lesser status of the warehouse; its position relates to the parapet of the State Theatre and the eaves of the flanking school building. The new façade will be a backcloth to the green zone that replaces Konrad Adenauer Strasse when the road goes underground. The ground surface will be landscaped with trees, paths and water canals; lightweight one-storey buildings will accommodate exhibitions, theatre displays, cafes and information. A single road on either side of the central zone will serve buildings on Konrad Adenauer Strasse along both sides of the 'Kulturmeile'.

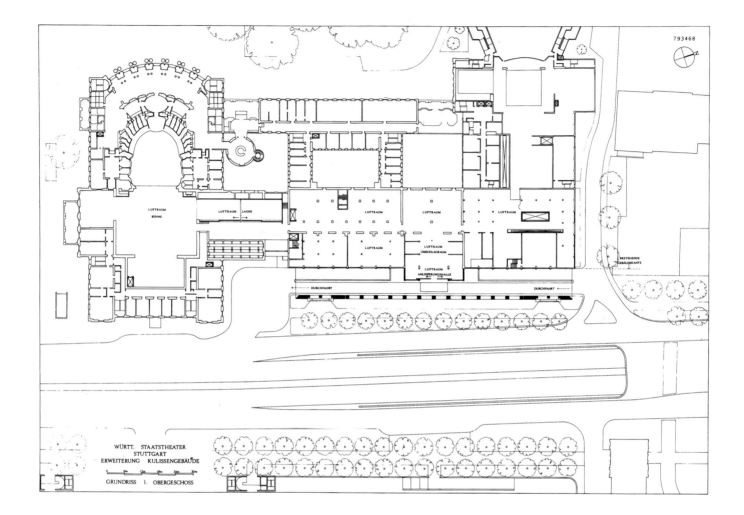

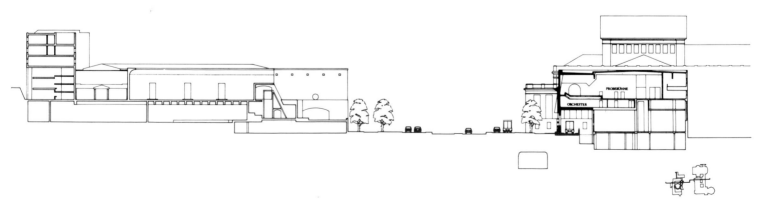

ABOVE: UPPER FLOOR PLAN; *BELOW*: CROSS SECTION

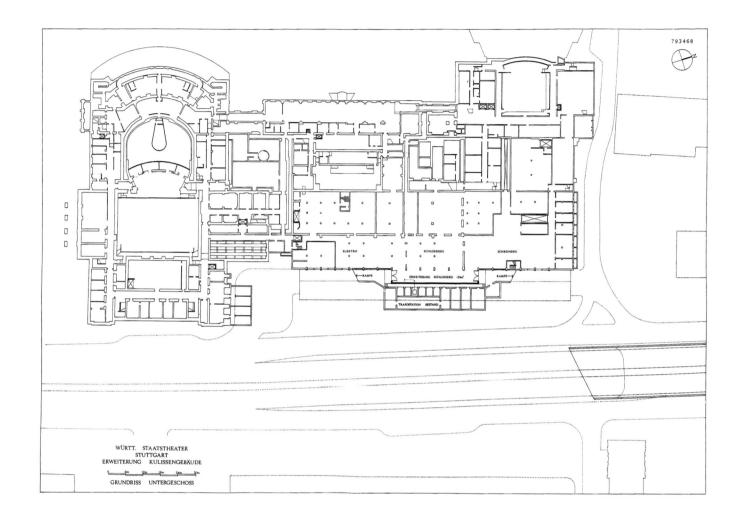

793468

WÜRTT. STAATSTHEATER
STUTTGART
ERWEITERUNG KULISSENGEBÄUDE

GRUNDRISS UNTERGESCHOSS

ELEKTRO   SCHLOSSEREI   SCHREINEREI
RAMPE   ERWEITERUNG SCHLOSSEREI 126m²   RAMPE
TRAFOSTATION BESTAND

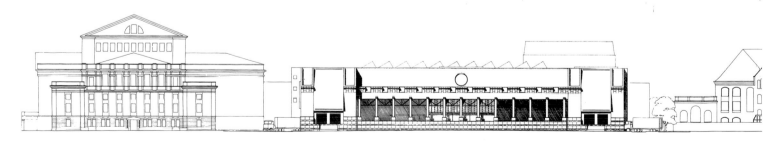

ABOVE: LOWER FLOOR PLAN; *BELOW*: ELEVATION

FACADE DETAIL

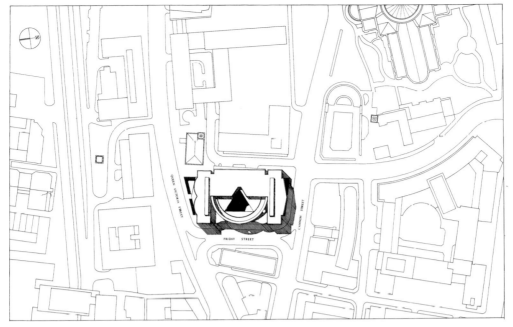

ABOVE: SITE PLAN; *BELOW*: AXONOMETRIC

BRACKEN HOUSE
CITY OF LONDON

Bracken House was designed by Sir Albert Richardson to house the printing presses and offices of the Financial Times. The redevelopment of the site south-east of St. Paul's Cathedral required an office building of 26,000m², to be built within the height restrictions imposed by the Cathedral. The inconsistency of floor heights made conversion impractical; partial demolition and conversion would have seriously diminished Richardson's design. Therefore we propose to rebuild over the whole site.

The irregular site is stabilised by vertical pillars at each corner, permitting a regular plan with rational and flexible office layouts. Stairways and services are contained in the corners. A light-well serves the central area of each level, allowing office floors to be either cellular or free-space. The top floor has a half-circular wall enclosing a roof garden and staff restaurants which have views into the garden. Fine quality bronze elements from the existing building will be incorporated into the new scheme.

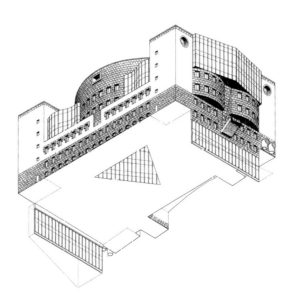

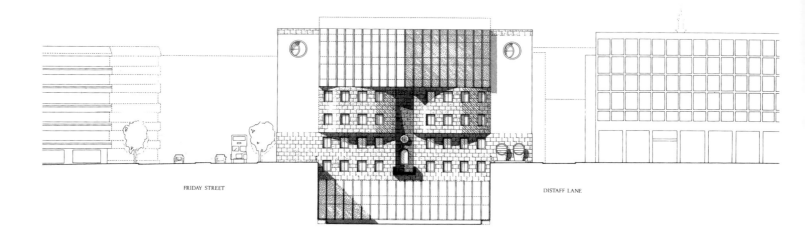

FRIDAY STREET   DISTAFF LANE

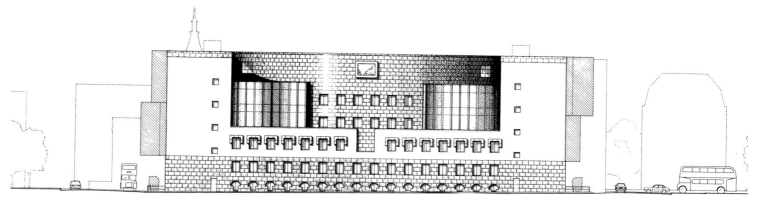

QUEEN VICTORIA STREET   CANNON STREET

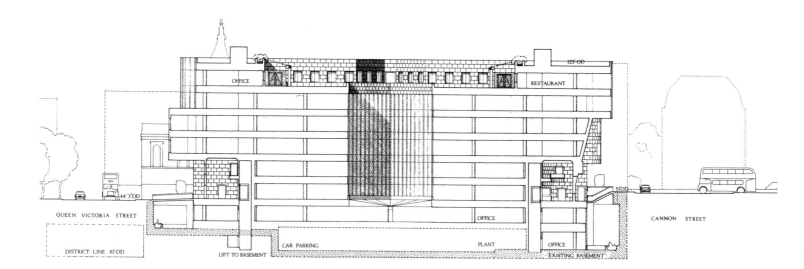

ABOVE: ELEVATIONS, *BELOW*: CROSS SECTION

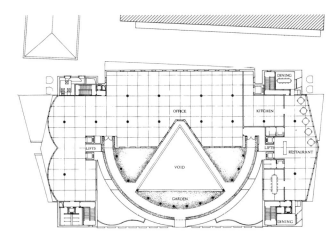

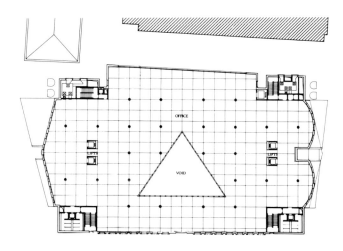

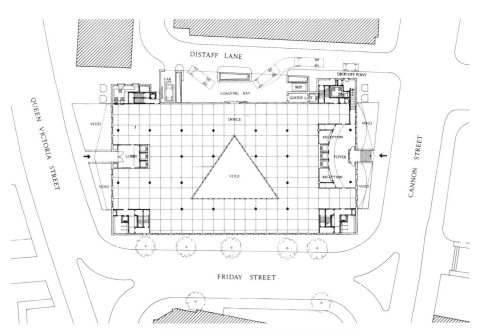

ABOVE: UPPER FLOOR PLAN; *BELOW*: LOWER FLOOR PLAN

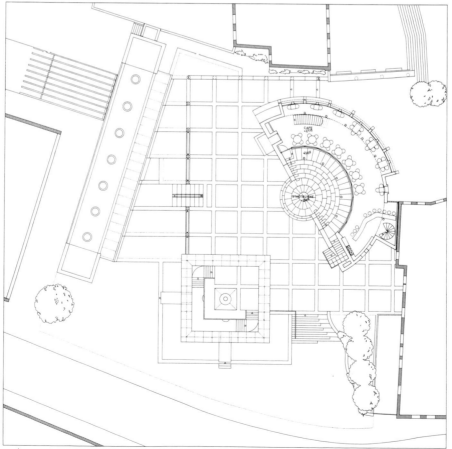

ABOVE: BASEMENT FLOOR PLAN; *BELOW*: SECOND LEVEL PLAN

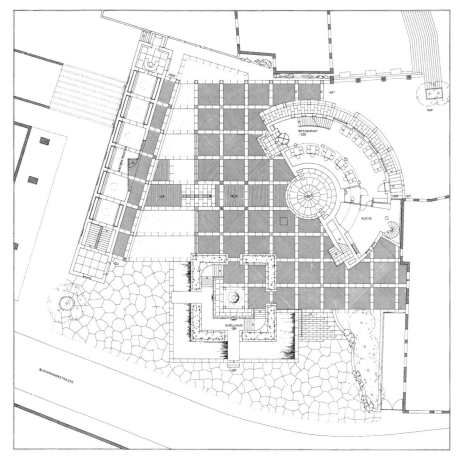

ABOVE: ENTRANCE LEVEL PLAN; *BELOW*: SITE SECTION

KAISERPLATZ
AACHEN, WEST GERMANY
Marlies Hentrup & Norbert Heyers with James Stirling

The project concerns the area of the former imperial spa, the Kaiserquelle, where the remains of a Roman military bath were found. The planning concept views it as a city centre resource, an inviting square reminding residents and visitors of the city's origin. The new facility is conceived around the frame of the old Roman structure, enclosed within four architectural elements, unified by choice of materials. The arcades are not intended as a reconstruction in the usual sense, but rather constitute an interpretation in material and form appropriate to the times. A semi-circular building establishes the boundary, limiting the paths over the square; only a narrow route remains through the existing and planned arcades, preserving the intimacy of the square. In the Spa House an artificial geyser makes the water gush loudly; a humidifier sends steam up and one can smell the sulphur of the hot water.*

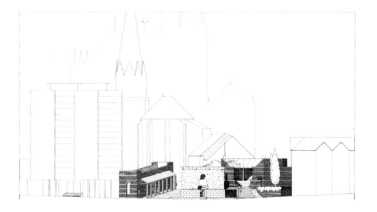

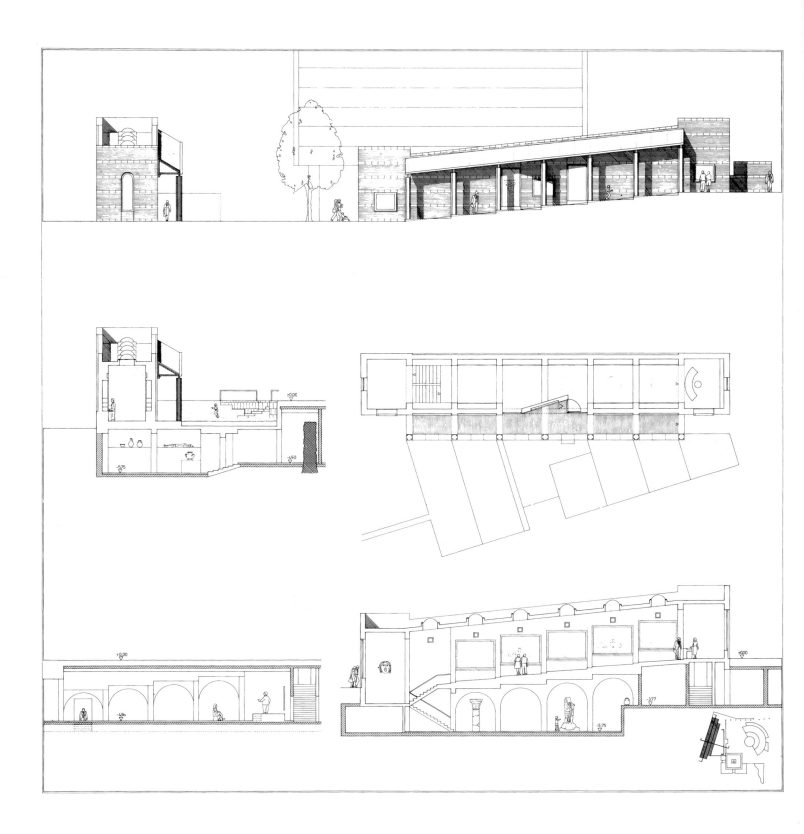

SITE AND BUILDING DETAILS

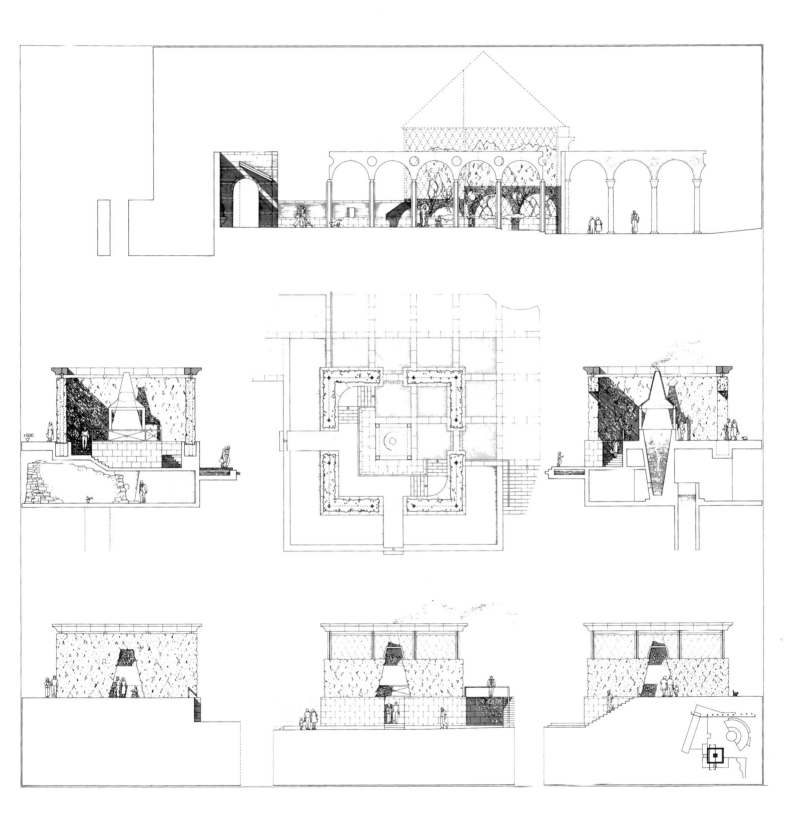

SITE AND BUILDING DETAILS

PERSPECTIVE VIEW

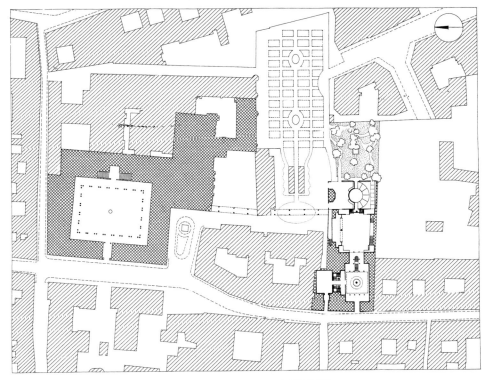

ABOVE: SITE PLAN; BELOW: BAR INTERIOR

PALAZZO CITTERIO ART GALLERY
BRERA MUSEUM, MILAN

Palazzo Citterio is an 18th-century patrician residence in the Barocchetto style. With its decorations and small garden it was representative of a period to which it remains an important testimony, particularly in the subdued curve of the façade following the bend of Via Brera. We were appointed to reorganise the building to a new programme, which forsees the Palazzo Citterio as a museum of international stature, with space for temporary exhibitions, a the display of 20th-century Italian art, and suites of rooms for donated collections. Modern facilities such as lecture-rooms, a bookshop and cafeteria, are also to be accomodated. The existing technical equipment will be upgraded to achieve environmental conditions suitable to international standards.

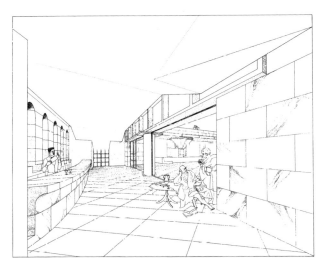

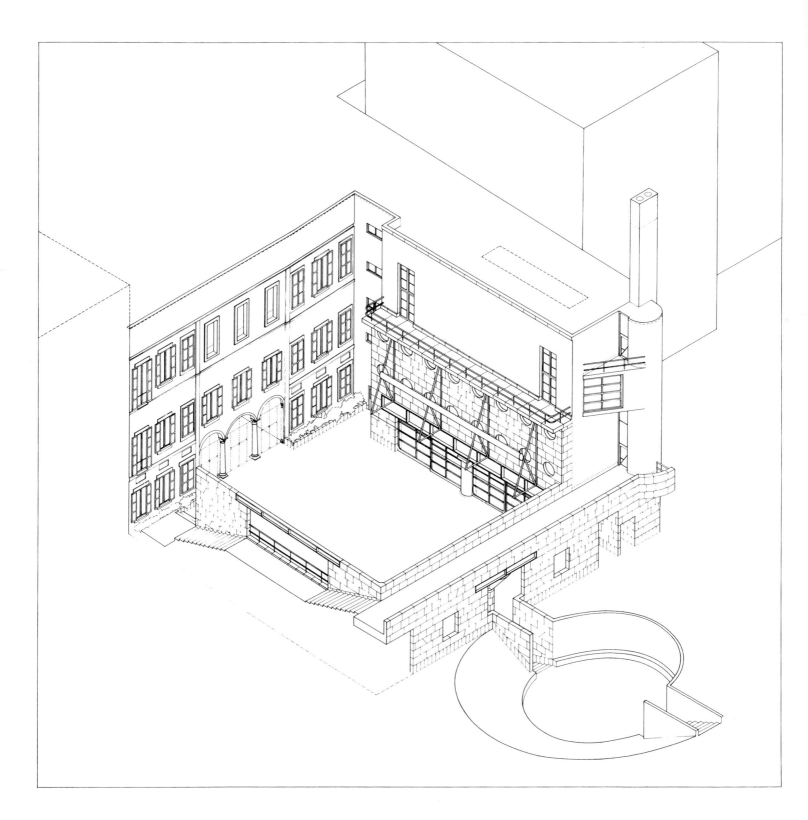

DISSECTED AXONOMETRIC

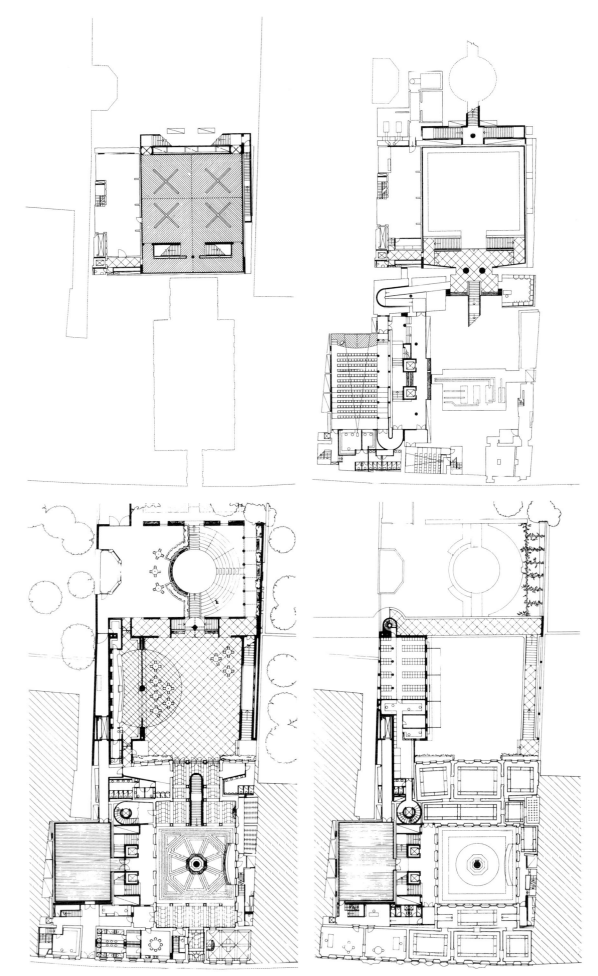

PLANS *ABOVE L TO R*: BASEMENT; LOWER GROUND; *BELOW L TO R*: UPPER GROUND; UPPER LEVEL

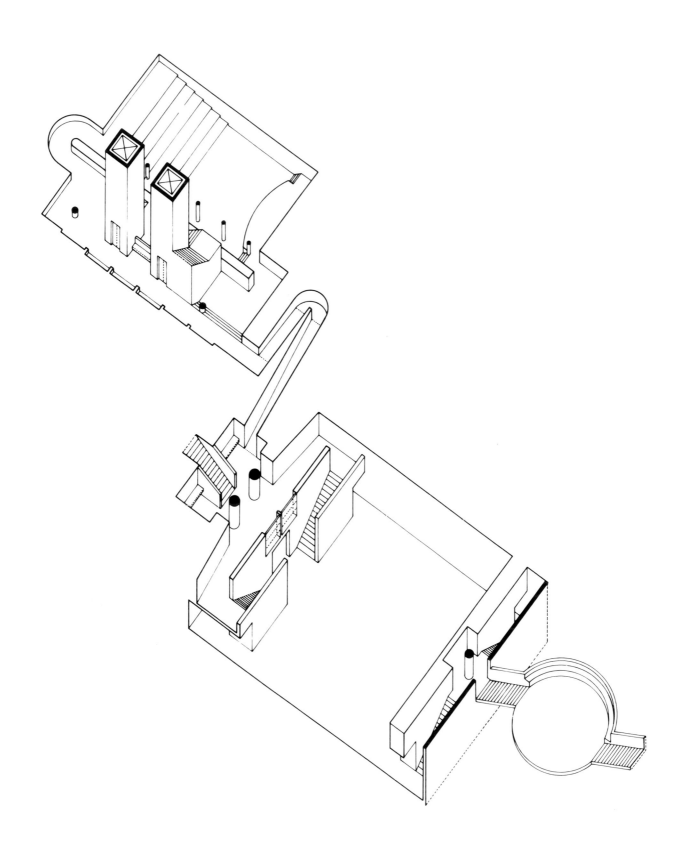

DISSECTED AXONOMETRIC

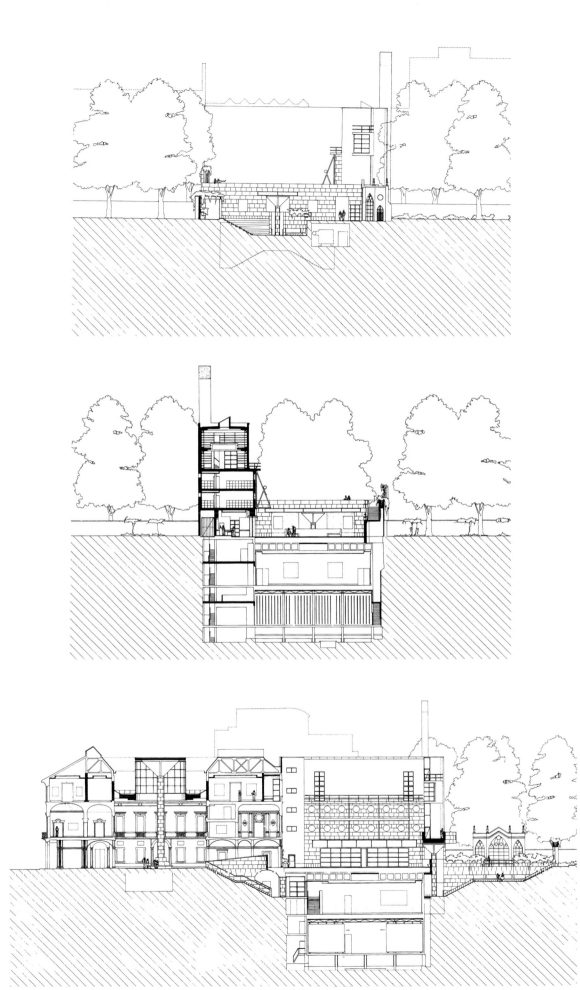

CROSS SECTIONS

COURTYARD IN WINTER

COURTYARD IN SUMMER

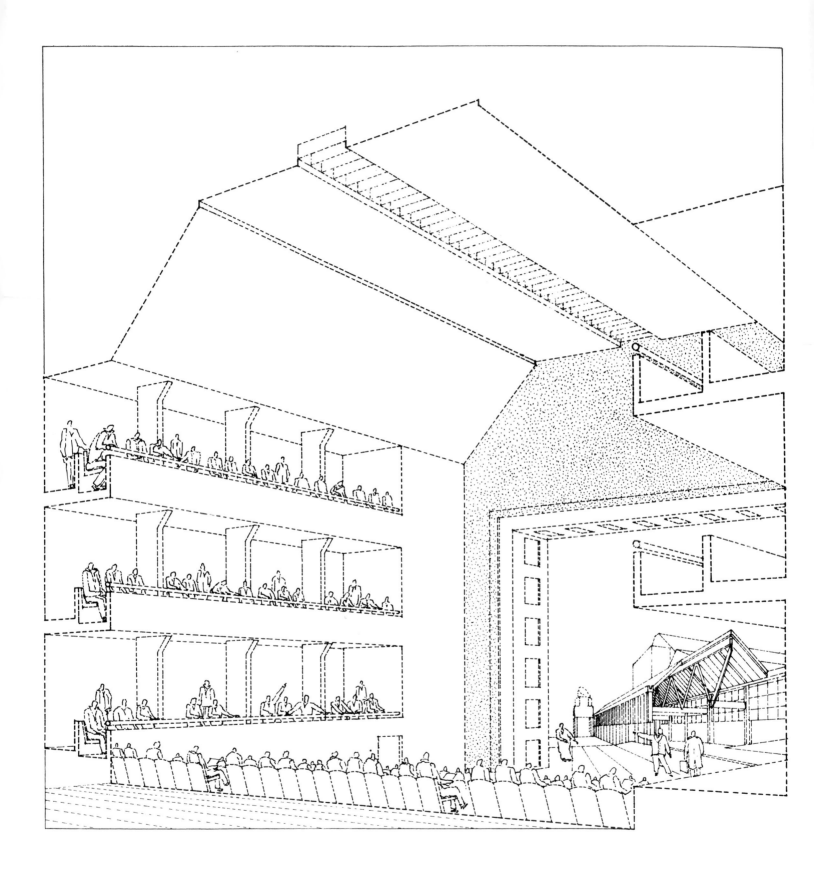

AUDITORIUM

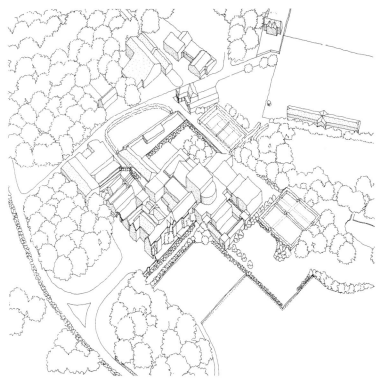

ABOVE: SKETCH AXONOMETRIC; *BELOW L TO R*: GROUND FLOOR PLAN, UPPER FLOOR PLAN

NEW OPERA HOUSE
GLYNDEBOURNE

The present opera house at Glyndebourne has its back to the gardens. The siting of the new opera house could reverse this, orienting public areas towards the landscape. The old auditorium and dressing room wing could be converted to accommodate restaurants. Cars entering the estate would be kept away from the house, directed via the service road to the existing carpark. Visitors would then approach through a new entrance pavilion and loggia overlooking the lake, gardens and landscape beyond. The loggia, constructed of stone and timber, would link new and old buildings, creating an open colonnade. The present auditorium would be replaced by a larger one, still maintaining the Glyndebourne character as distinct from urban Operas. The proposal would allow the use of facilities during the closed season.

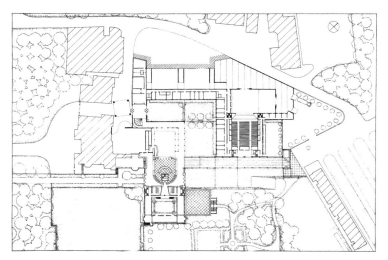
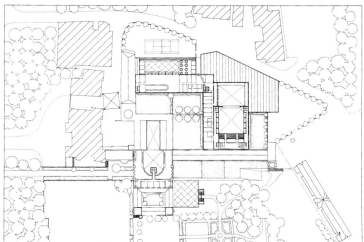

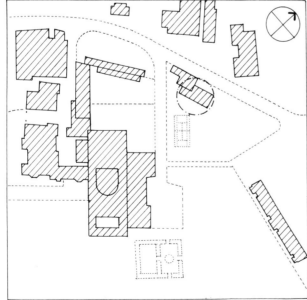

THE SITE. The old stables (circled) will be repositioned possibly close to the lake for picnicers.

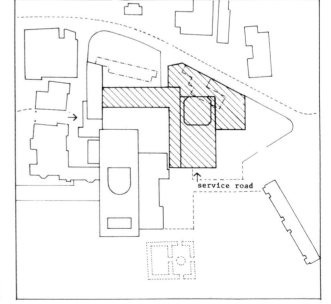

PHASE 1. The construction of the new opera house, dressing room and administration will be completed while performances continue in the existing auditorium. A temporary service road will connect the existing road and loading area.

ABOVE: PARTIAL PERSPECTIVE; *BELOW L TO R*: SITE PLAN, CONSTRUCTION PHASE DIAGRAM

PHASE 2. The existing auditorium will become
the restaurants replacing the Wallop Halls.
The loggia will allow easy access from the
car park. In winter this entrance could be
used by visitors to the restaurant
minimising noise at the house.

DELIVERIES to the stage will be along the
existing road entering the loading area
from the car park.

ABOVE: RESTAURANT INTERIOR; *BELOW L TO R*: CONSTRUCTION PHASE DIAGRAM, DELIVERIES DIAGRAM

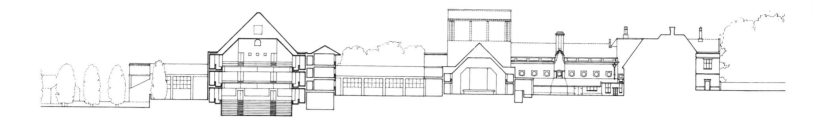

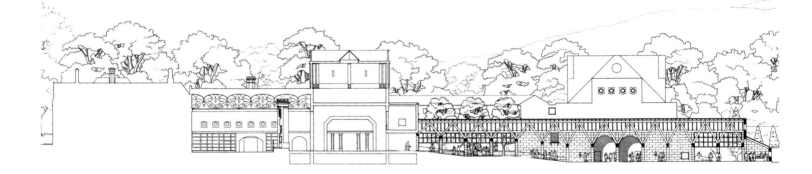

ABOVE: CROSS SECTIONS; *BELOW*: ELEVATION

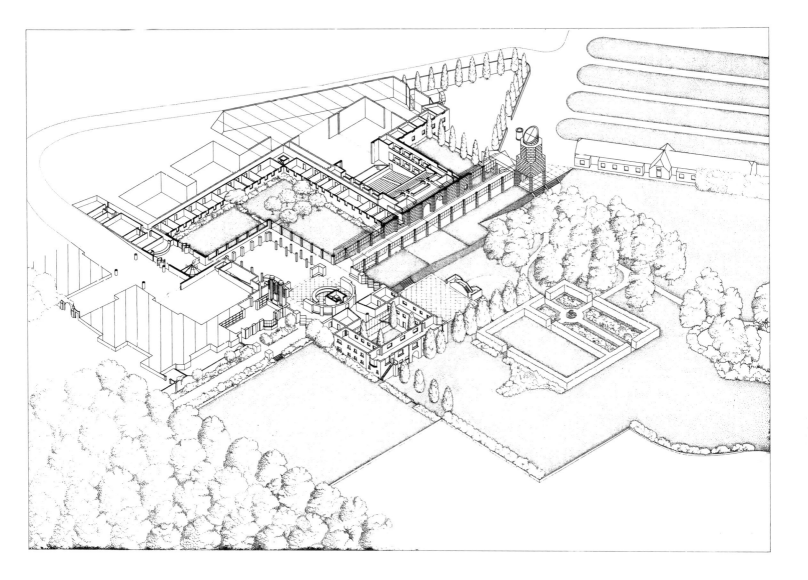

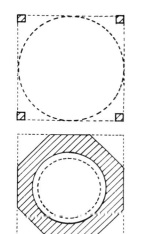
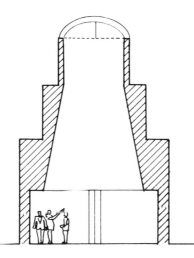
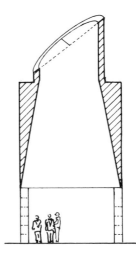
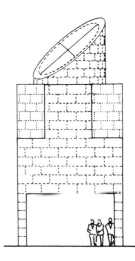

ABOVE: PARTIAL SITE ISOMETRIC; *BELOW*: LIGHT TOWER DIAGRAMS

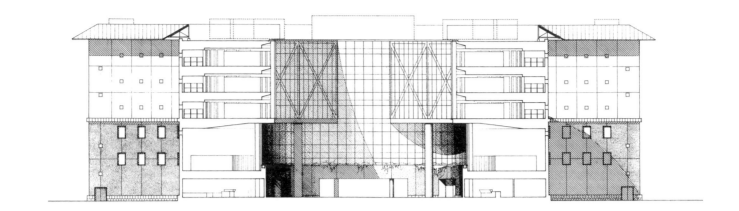

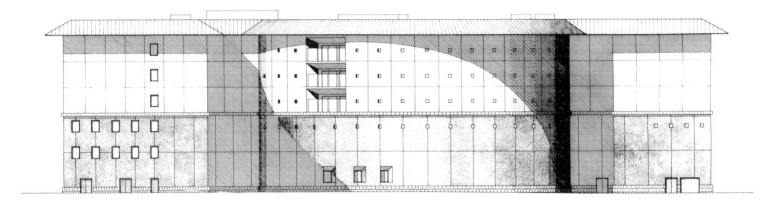

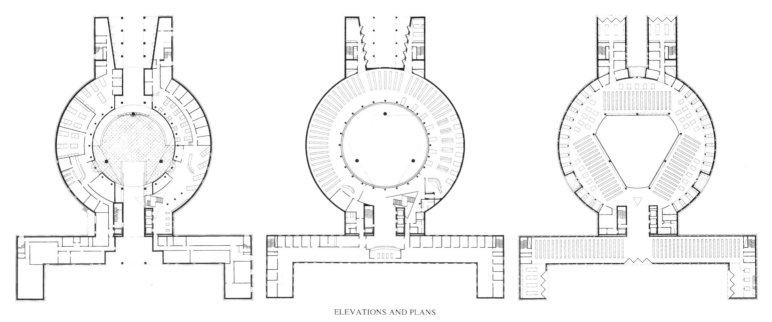

ELEVATIONS AND PLANS

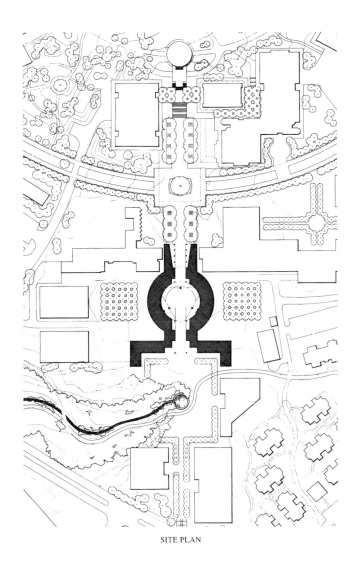

SITE PLAN

SCIENCE LIBRARY, UNIVERSITY OF CALIFORNIA
IRVINE, LOS ANGELES

The library will be a campus landmark and centrepiece for the Sciences. Highly visible from all around, it doubles as a gateway to the plaza and a portal to the biological sciences quadrangle. The circular courtyard will be experienced by passers-by as well as users, functioning both as the entrance to the library and a place to meet friends. The entrance colonnade is first in a sequence of contracting and expanding spaces. Splayed walls focus on the central courtyard encouraging passage into and through the building, which opens onto a tree-lined square incorporating the existing arroyo and redwood grove. This spatial progression ensures an attractive promenade between the ring-mall and the medical school, reducing the apparent length of the biological sciences mall

which is the longest on campus. The central court allows the entrances to be located at the heart of the building and provides an allround light source to the interior. The form centres the architectural composition and allows the building to face in different directions – a gateway to the ring-mall and a wide embracing façade towards the medical school. Over 2,000 reader places are provided, accommodation being arranged on six floors. Entry is at grade via the central courtyard. Three passenger elevators, one staff/freight elevator and five staircases provide vertical circulation. The building has a stucco finish with sandstone base and string courses. Overhanging eaves conceal the service plant on the roof. Construction will be completed in 1992.

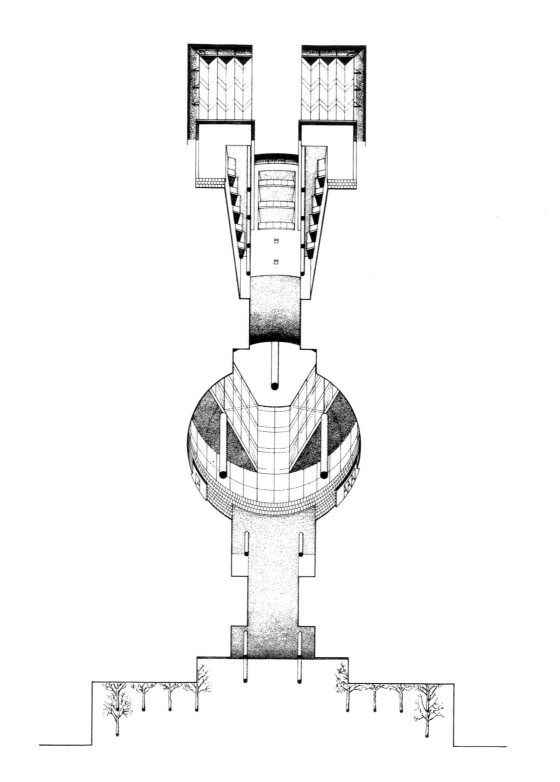

AXONOMETRIC

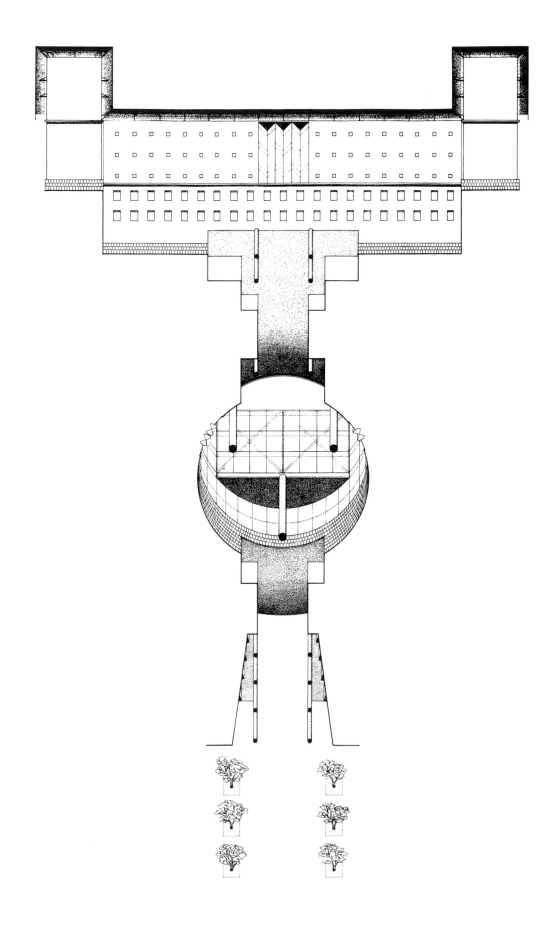

AXONOMETRIC

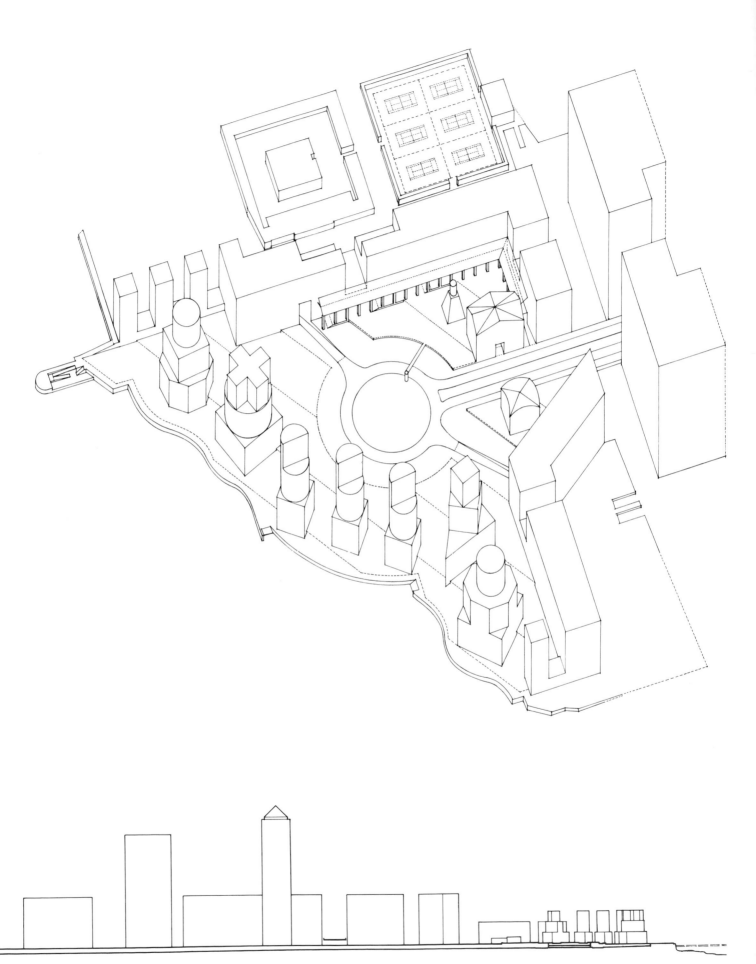

ABOVE: SITE AXONOMETRIC; *BELOW*: CROSS SECTION

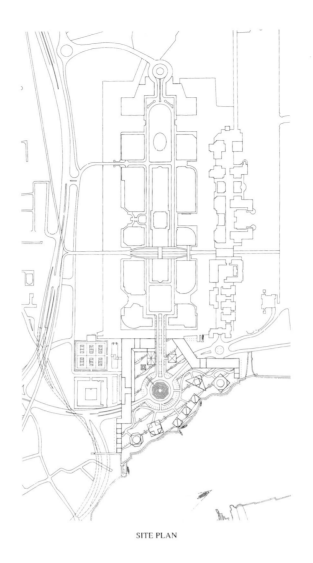

SITE PLAN

RESIDENTIAL DEVELOPMENT
CANARY WHARF, LONDON

In response to the developer's land use reappraisal our alternative design proposes a large riverside park with terraces stepping down to the Thames. This garden is semi-enclosed on the inland sides by linear buildings containing offices, retail spaces and a hotel. The new park will contain apartment towers ranged informally along the river front. The park surrounds the existing West Ferry Circus, a large roundabout which, together with its approach roads, will be incised into the stepped terraces. The airy spaciousness of the park will provide a contrast with the commercial core of Canary Wharf; it combines public and private open spaces, accessible as appropriate to residents, office workers and the adjacent communities. The new park will create an interesting 'gateway' to Canary Wharf, the varied building forms with their reflective glass surfaces creating a dramatic river-front on the Thames. Residents, office workers and visitors could enjoy garden walks, picnics and impromptu events on these terraces. The residents of towers would enjoy views of the Thames. A loggia overlooking the park contains pubs, restaurants and shops with access to the perimeter office buildings. The site planning of individual buildings allows flexibility with the investment and implementation. Each building has its own parking and services infrastructure, which could be constructed independently for each tower. Consequently the development could be phased, and constructed over a period of time.

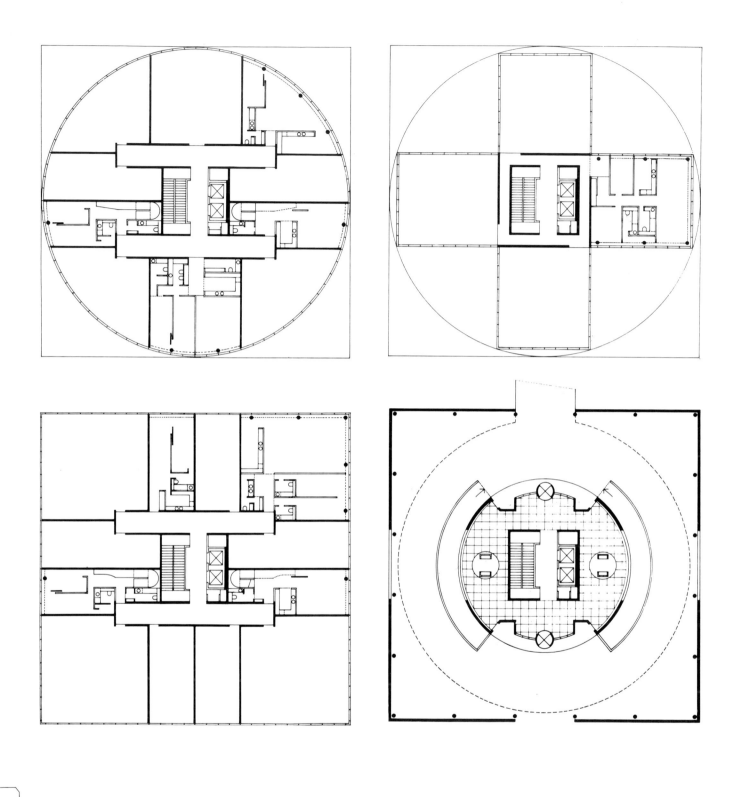

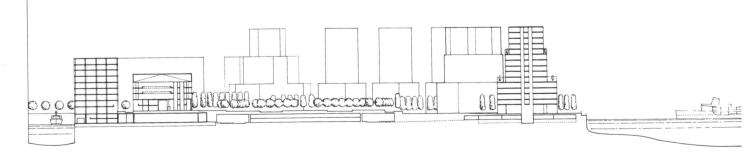

ABOVE: TOWER FLOOR PLANS; *BELOW*: SITE SECTION

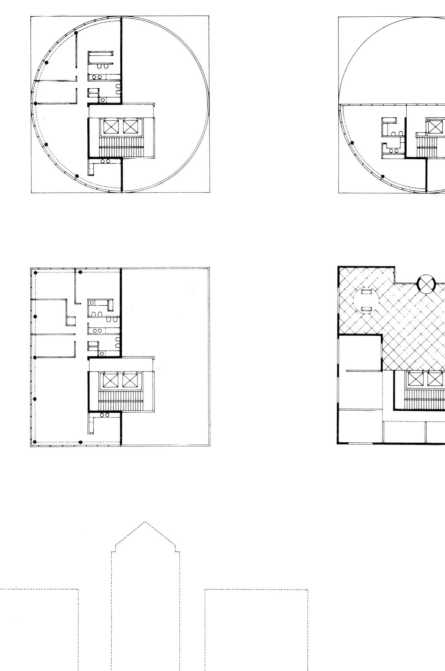

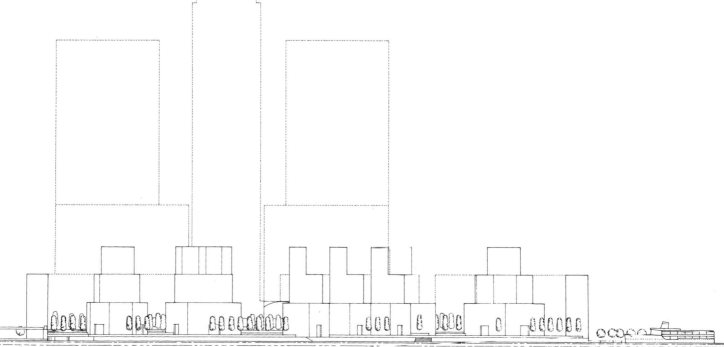

ABOVE: TOWER FLOOR PLANS; *BELOW*: SITE SECTION

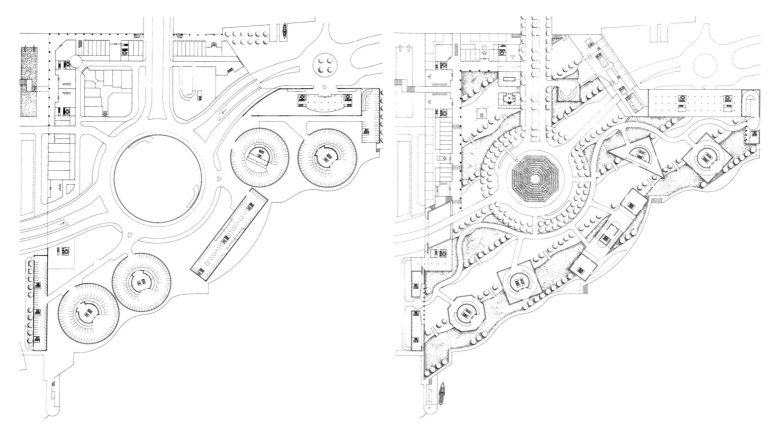

ABOVE: ORIGINAL SCHEME BY SOM; *BELOW L TO R*: BASEMENT PLAN, GROUND FLOOR PLAN

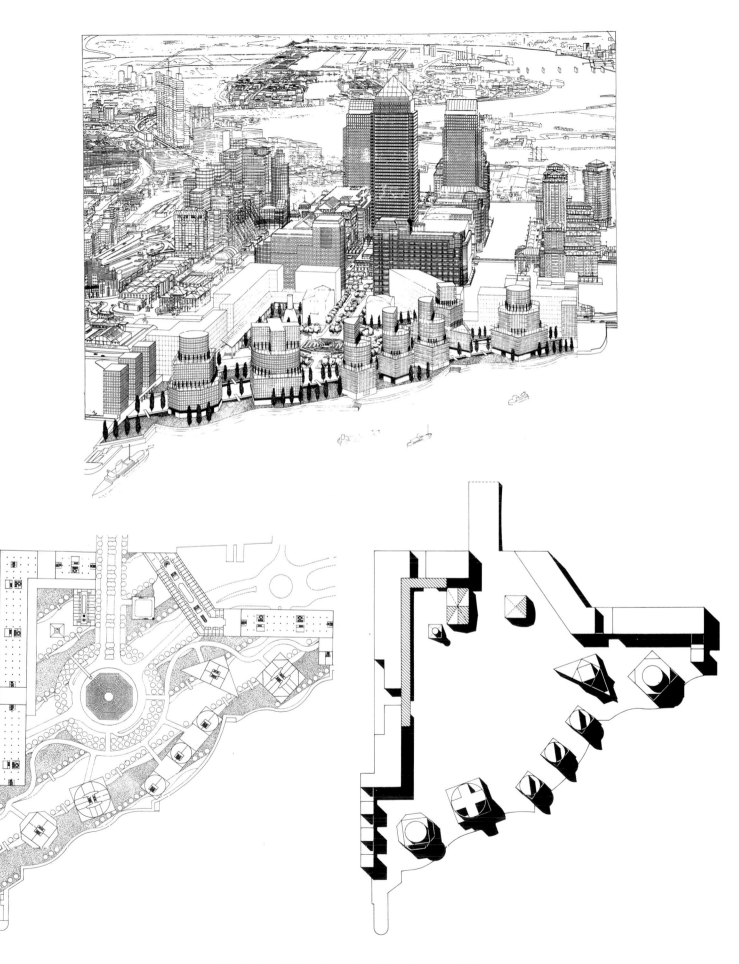

ABOVE: SITE PERSPECTIVE; *BELOW L TO R*: UPPER FLOOR PLAN, ROOF PLAN

ABOVE: ROOF PLAN; *BELOW*: MODEL PHOTOGRAPH, DETAIL

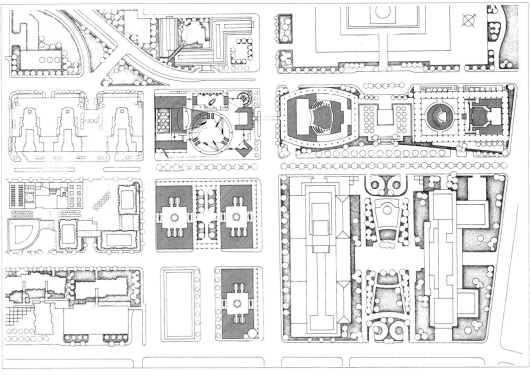

ABOVE: SITE PLAN; BELOW: CONCERT HALL SEATING PLANS

LOS ANGELES PHILHARMONIC HALL
LOS ANGELES

We hope to achieve a civic identity for the Walt Disney Concert Hall that is both in the tradition of monumental public buildings and a populist place of culture and entertainment. Our design is an ensemble of architectural forms related to the functional elements of the programme, unified at ground level by a grand concourse. The disposition of the elements is informal, yet geometrically related to the north/south axis of the music centre. The circular, stepped concert hall is the centrepiece of the composition. The infor- *mality of the concourse with its performance and intermission activities contrasts with the calm ambience of the concert and chamber music halls. Bars and lounges overlook Hope Street, facing downtown through bay windows. The Grand Reception Hall is a spacious double-height room with large windows overlooking the garden. External materials would be glass and stone, perhaps red sandstone similar to that at M.O.C.A. Stone could also be applied to the faceted surfaces of the Concert Hall within the concourse.*

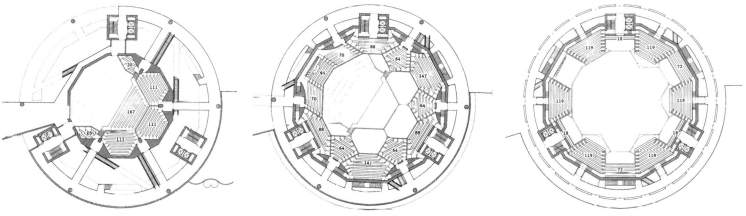

81

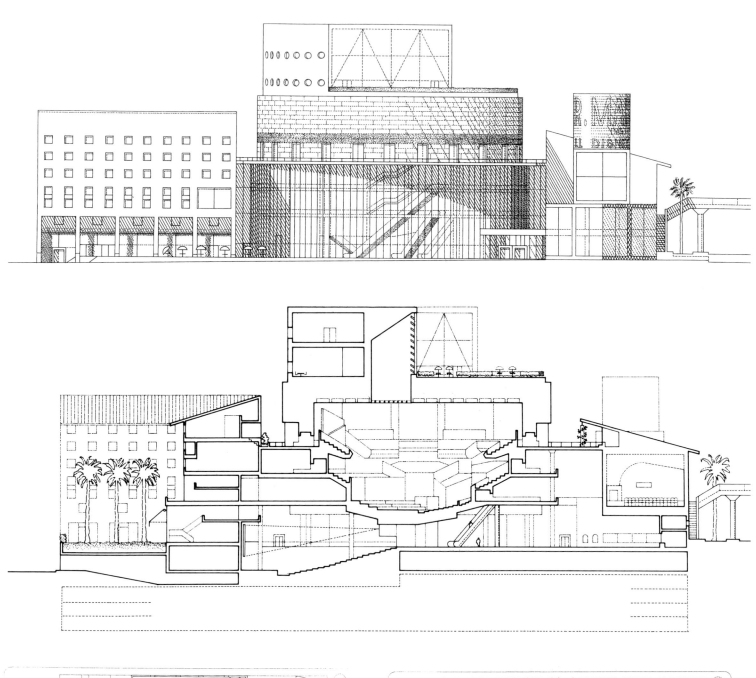

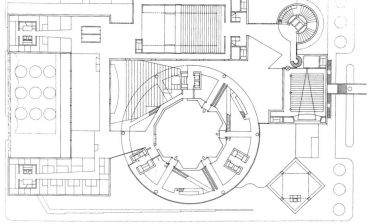
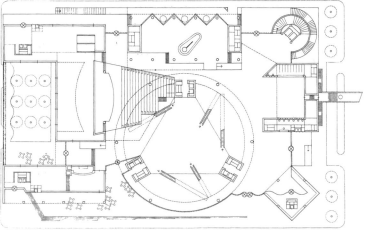

ABOVE: GRAND AVENUE ELEVATION; *CENTRE*: CONCERT HALL SECTION; *BELOW L TO R*:THIRD LEVEL PLAN, ENTRANCE LEVEL PLAN

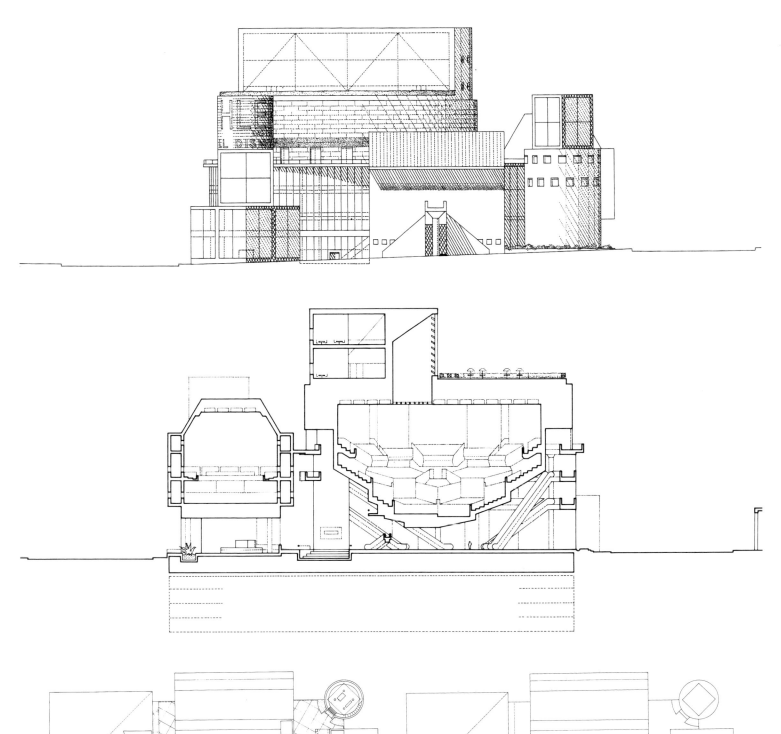

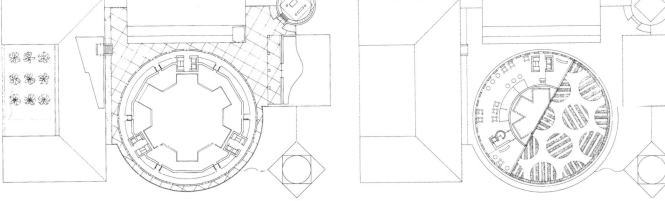

ABOVE: FIRST STREET ELEVATION; *CENTRE*: CROSS SECTION; *BELOW l. TO R*: FOURTH LEVEL PLAN, GARDEN LEVEL PLAN

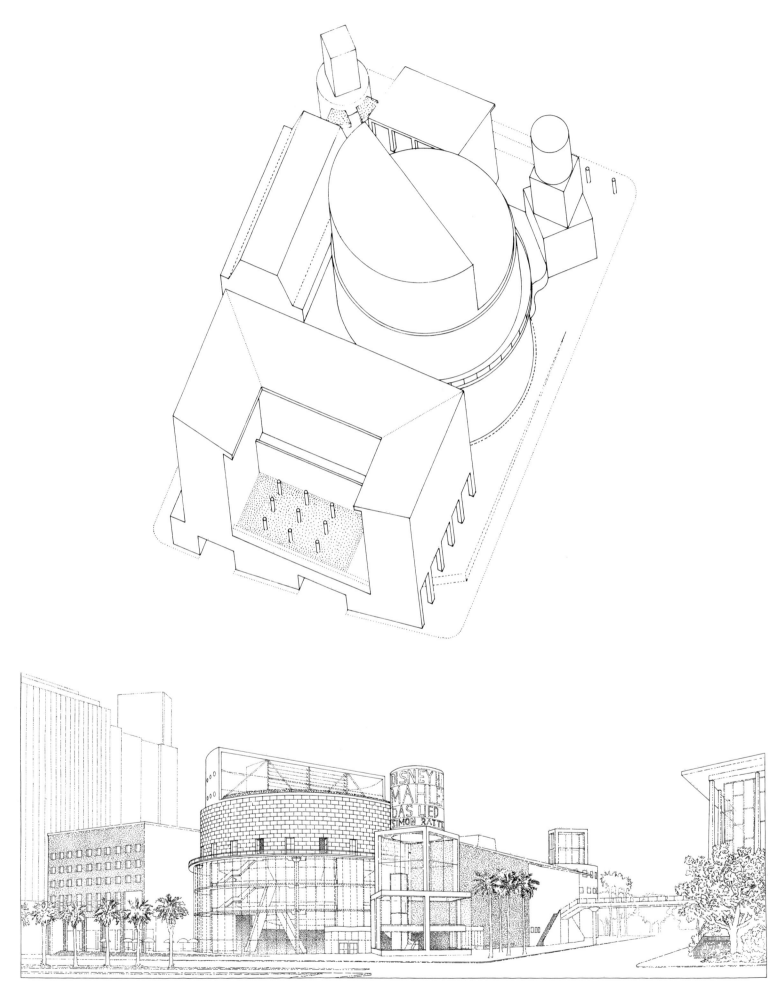

ABOVE: SITE AXONOMETRIC; *BELOW*: PERSPECTIVE VIEW

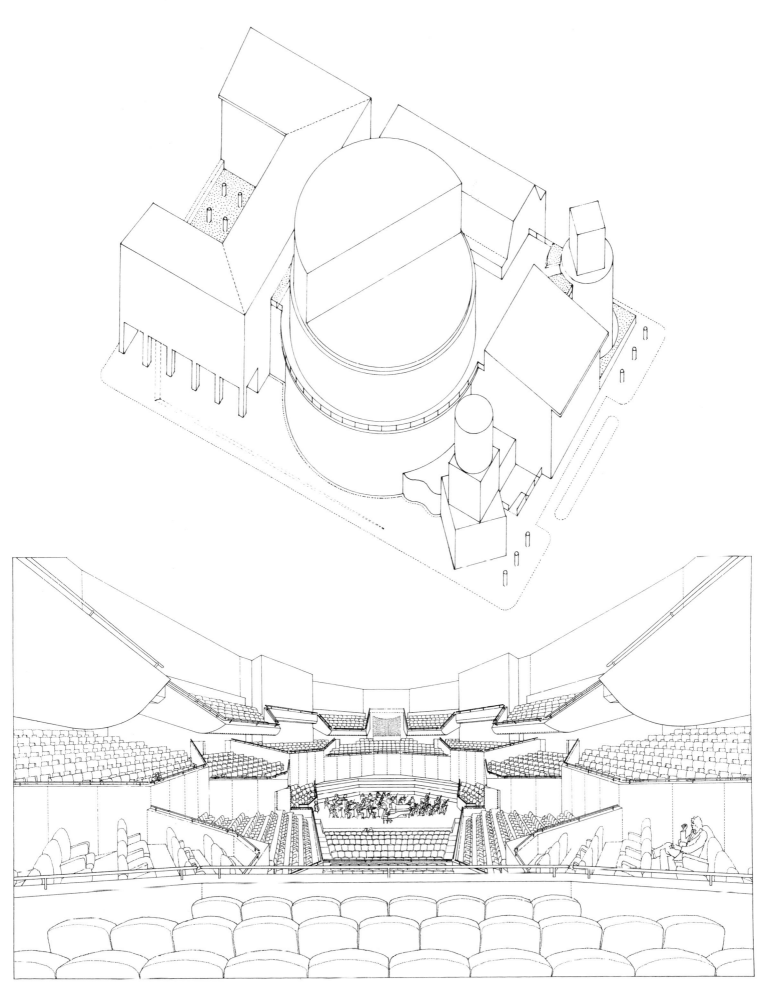

ABOVE: SITE AXONOMETRIC; *BELOW*: INTERIOR PERSPECTIVE

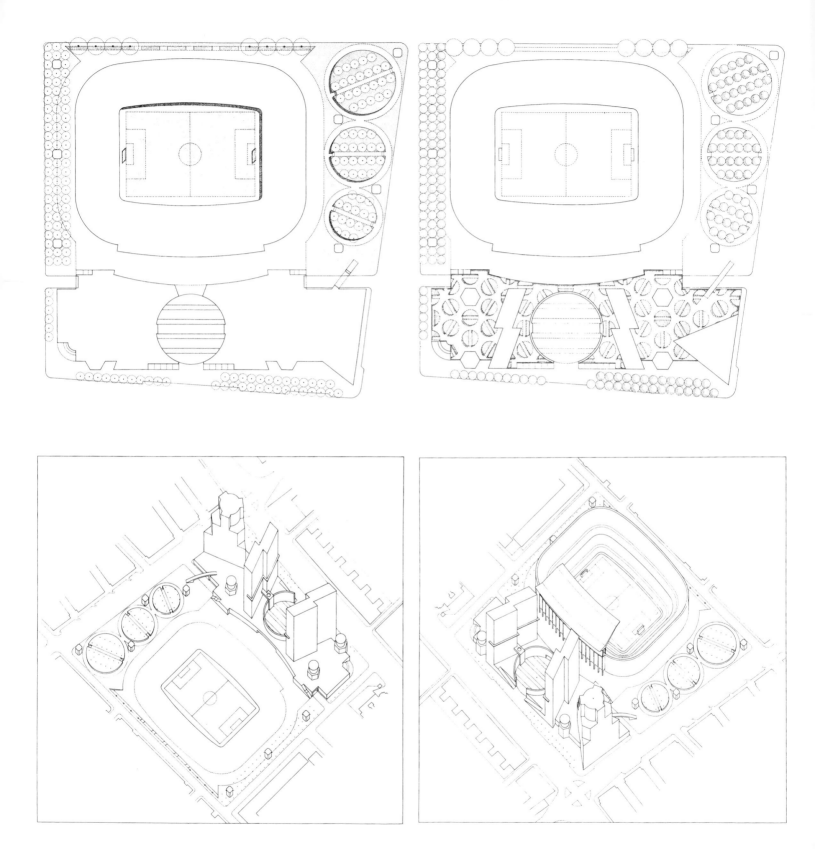

ABOVE: SITE PLANS; *BELOW*: SITE AXONOMETRICS

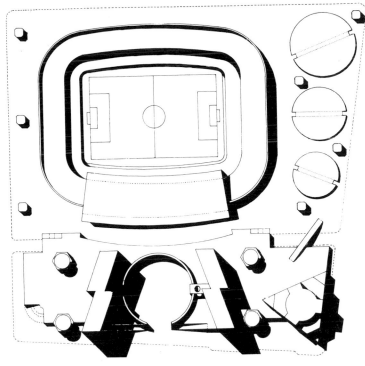

ABOVE: ROOF PLAN; BELOW: MODEL PHOTOGRAPH

STADIUM DEVELOPMENT
SEVILLE

For the development of vacant ground we propose a series of public gardens with three buildings and four pavilions. Along the Calle Luis Morales a raised podium defines the street, embracing a large circular 'placa' through which mass crowds pass en route to the football stadium. The west (front) side of this stadium is the more important, accomodating the best seats under a large roof canopy. Consequently the public open space is located here. On the vacant south side, three circular gardens with shady trees allowing access to the stadium are slightly raised to protect them from the mass crowds on football days. The remaining two sides of the stadium have avenues of *trees. On the podium two 12-storey office buildings are positioned either side of the circular 'placa'. A mid-level cornice corresponds with the cantilevered edge of the stadium canopy. A 280-room Hotel also sits on the podium, the flank of which compositionally relates the podium and office buildings to the circular gardens. Cross paths through these gardens restate the radial composition of buildings and gardens around the stadium. Within the raised podium is a Department Store. The four octagonal pavilions have splayed rooflights providing daylight to the entrances and atriums where escalators descend to the basement.*

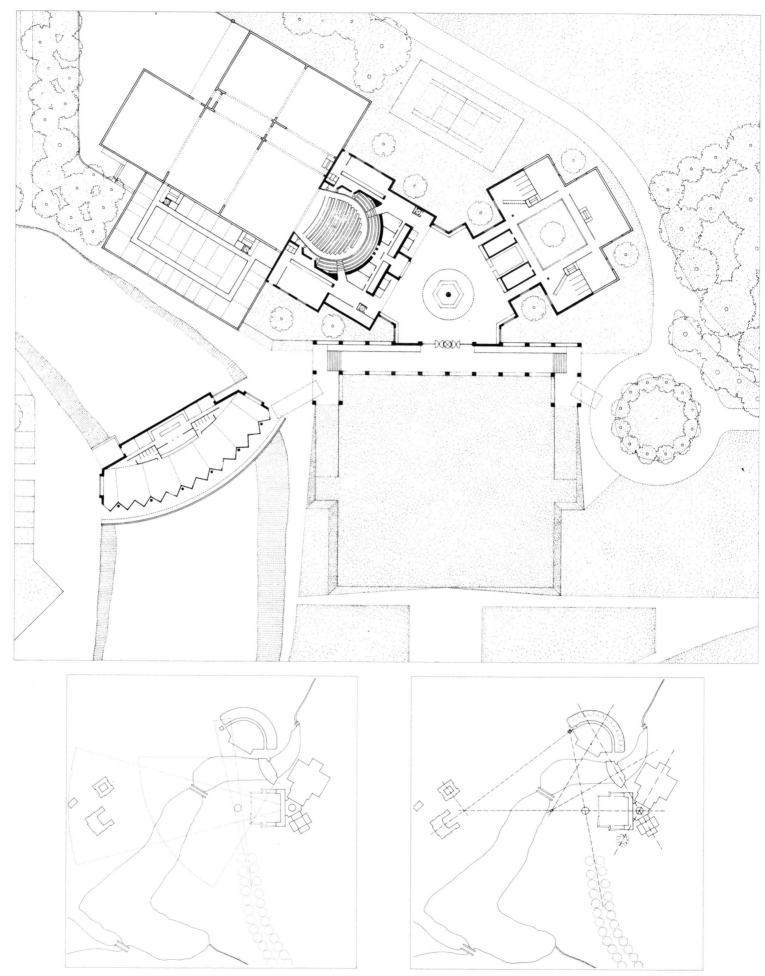

ABOVE: FIRST FLOOR PLAN; *BELOW L TO R*: VISTAS & VIEWS, BUILDING AXES

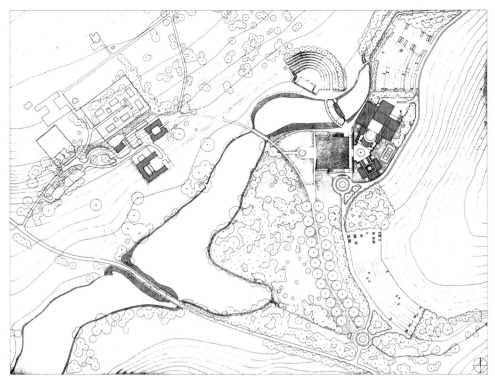

ABOVE: SITE PLAN; BELOW: MODEL PHOTOGRAPH

COMPTON VERNEY
OPERA HOUSE

Soil investigations showing limestone just below the surface made proposals to sink the building into the ground difficult and expensive. Consequently we have reduced the apparent height of the stagehouse by the forward positioning of the loggia, the administration pavilion and the restaurant bridge. Viewed from the mansion house and across the lake, the auditorium and stagehouse will recede in perspective behind a foreground of loggia and restaurant bridge. The loggia allows visitors to approach from all directions, forming a backdrop to the lawn. The administration pavilion encloses a garden court. The restaurant bridges the lake, with a footway connecting the loggia to the garden amphitheatre. In fine weather, car and bus passengers would disembark at the gatehouse and walk into the grounds. The curved sequoia avenue forms a natural approach from the south, drawing visitors towards the lawn and entrance loggia. Walking down the avenue, dramatic views of the Adam bridge, the lake and the mansion house would gradually come into view. The new buildings are arranged as pavilions and follies around the end of the lake suggesting picturesque and formal relationships between the buildings and the landscape.

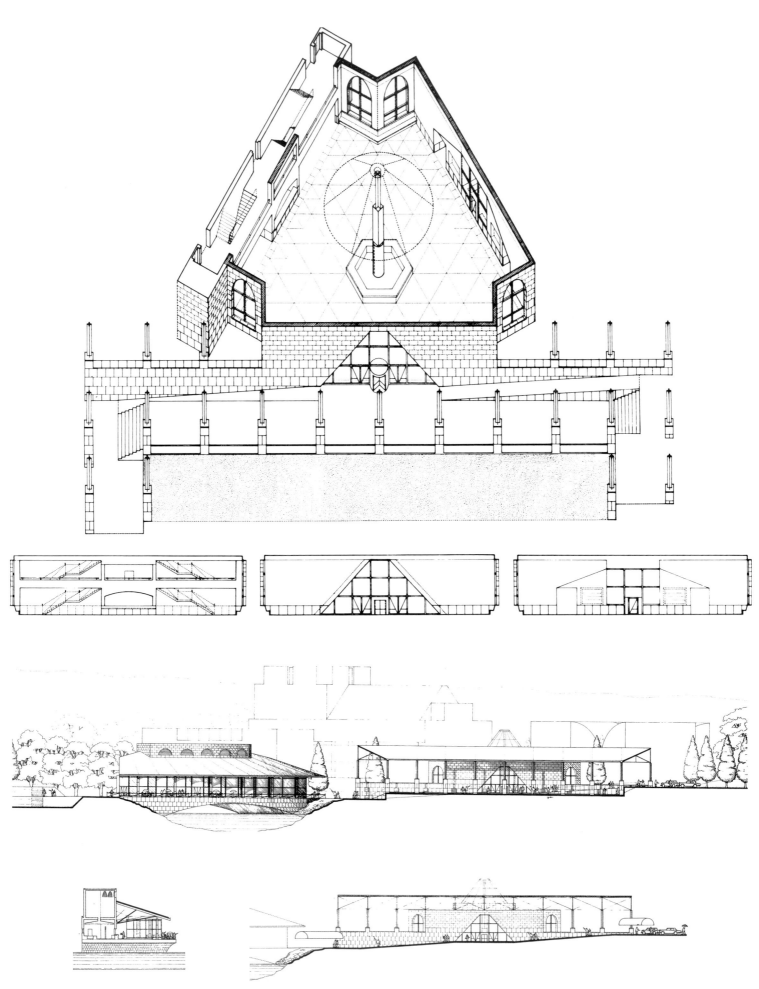

ABOVE: AXONOMETRIC OF LOGGIA AND ENTRANCE HALL; *CENTRE*: ELEVATION *BELOW L TO R*: RESTAURANT SECTION , LOGGIA ELEVATION

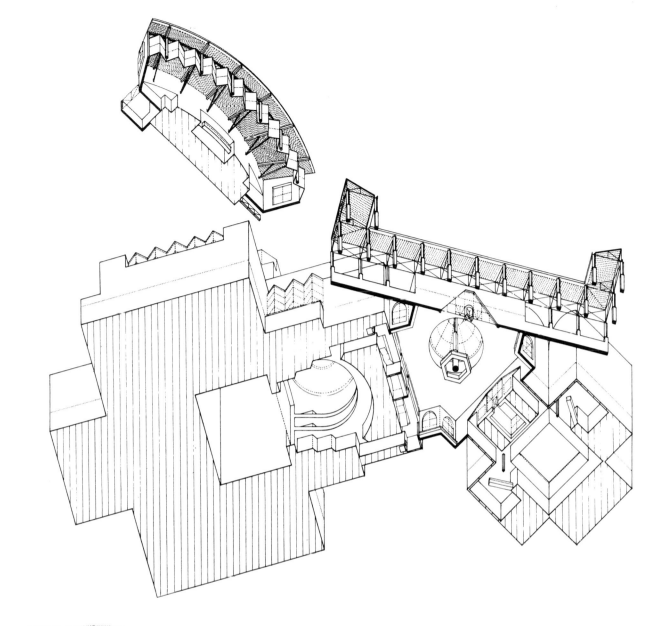

ABOVE: WORM'S EYE AXONOMETRIC; *BELOW*: PERSPECTIVE

SITE AXONOMETRIC

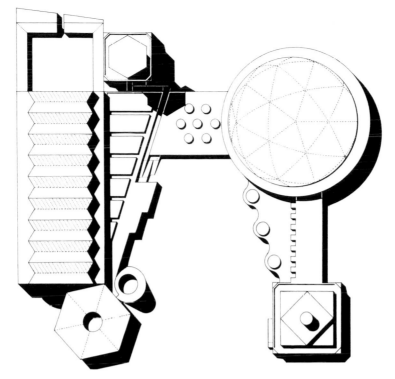

ABOVE: ROOF PLAN; *BELOW*: MODEL PHOTOGRAPH

BIBLIOTHÈQUE DE FRANCE
PARIS

Our proposal for the Bibliothèque de France is conceived as a 'grouping' of buildings around a new public park, an open garden rising in stepped terraces from the River Seine to the main entrance. This concept allows each of the four libraries its own separate identity and avoids an unattractive 'Kafka-esque' experience, which such a large building could produce if planned as a single volume. The new footbridge across the Seine will relate to the park, allowing panoramic views of the new buildings. Three elements of the library – the dome, the vault and the tower – rise above the general level, enlivening the skyline of the Tolbiac Quarter. Internally the library is planned around a 'U' shaped concourse. From the entrance, at the heart of the plan, this concourse flows westwards through the domed recent acquisitions library, passing the Café Europe en route to the sound and moving image library which is on the edge of the Seine. The open concourse encourages a sense of exploration and discovery. It has transitions in scale, and changes in ambience, from the transparent public activities surrounding the park, which include shops and restaurants, to the private study areas of the libraries.

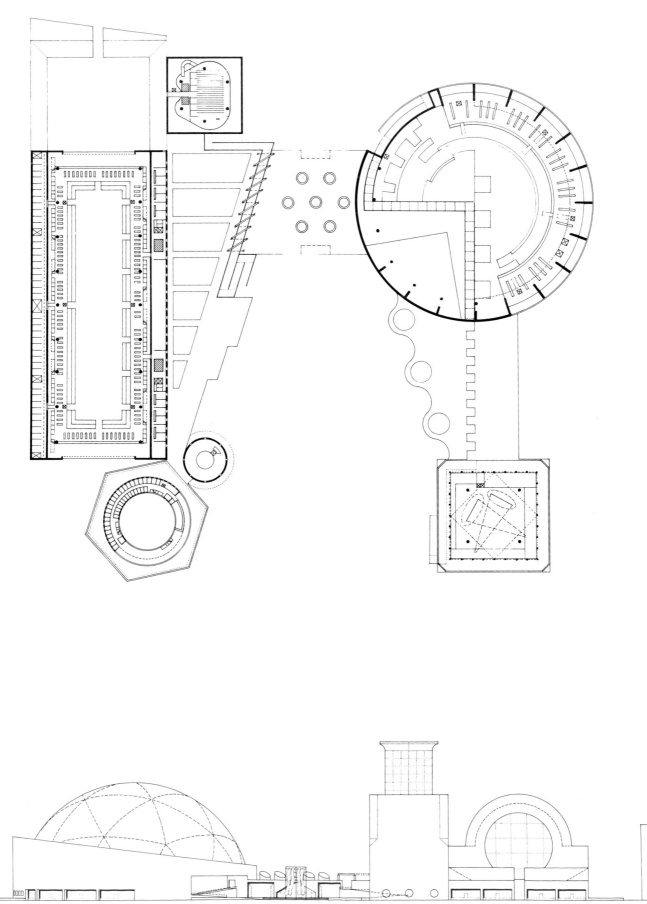

ABOVE: FOURTH LEVEL PLAN; *BELOW*: ELEVATION

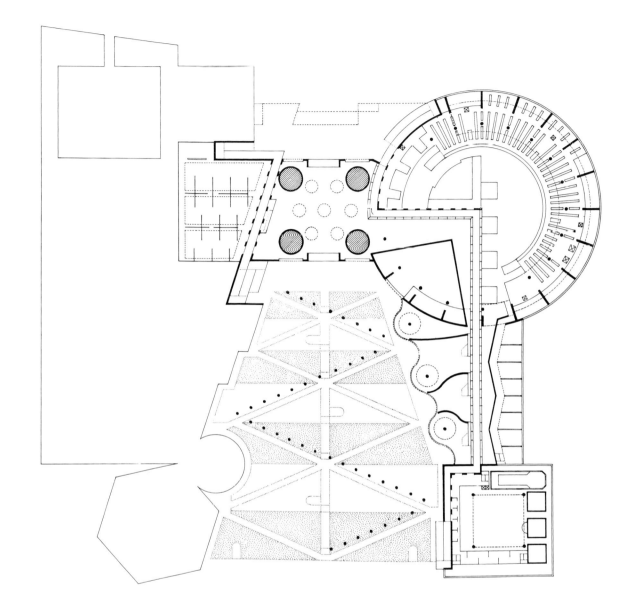

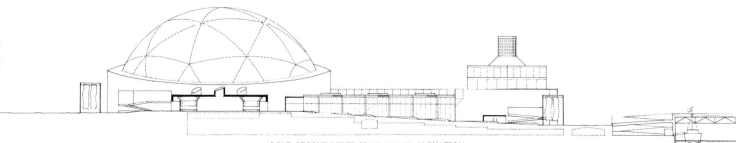

ABOVE: SECOND LEVEL PLAN; *BELOW*: ELEVATION

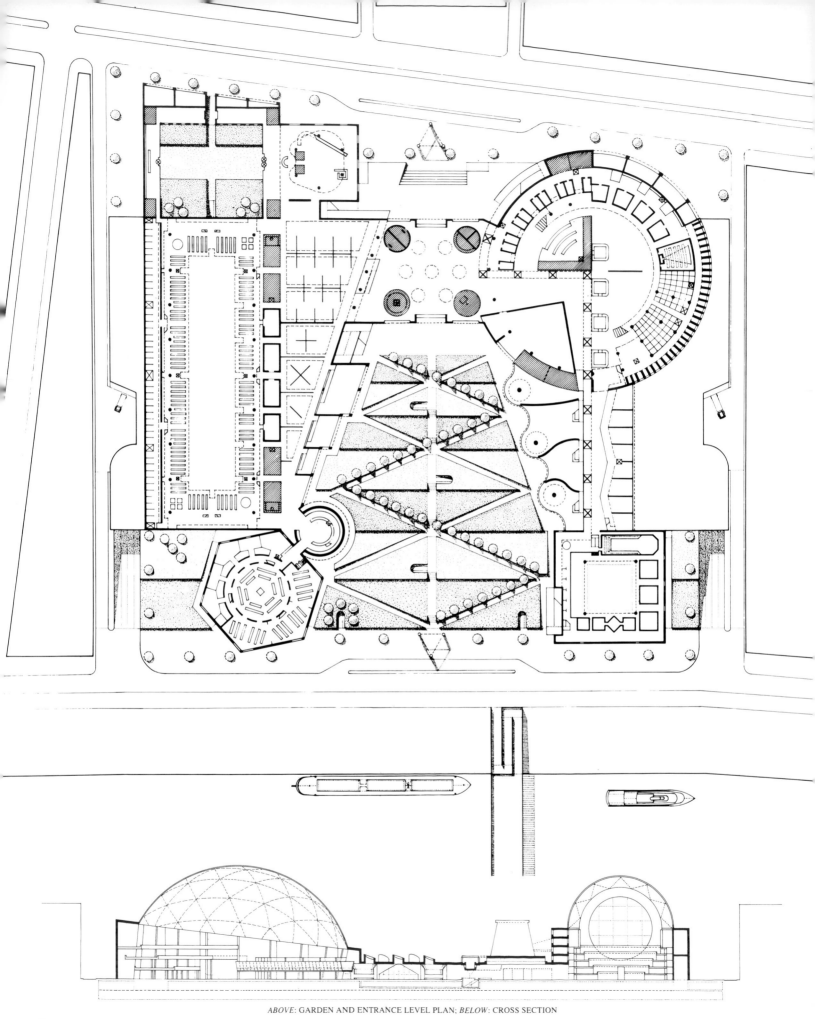

ABOVE: GARDEN AND ENTRANCE LEVEL PLAN; *BELOW*: CROSS SECTION

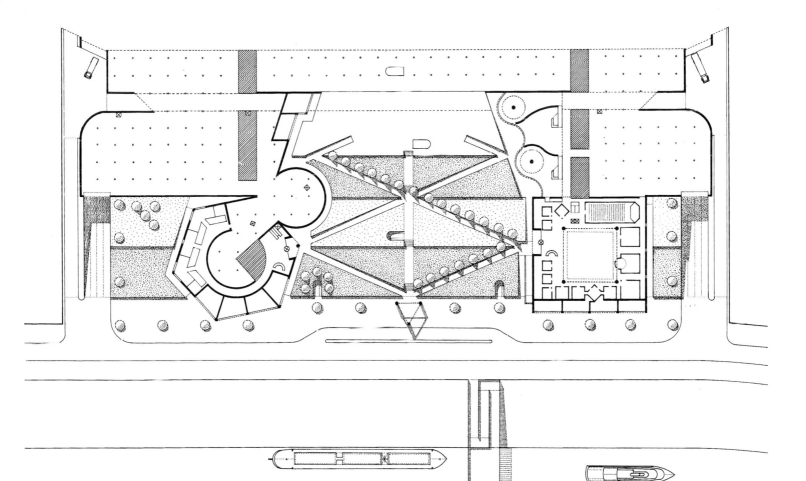

ABOVE: DETAIL OF ENTRANCE LEVEL PLAN; *CENTRE & BELOW*: ELEVATIONS

ABOVE: VIEW INTO RESTAURANT FROM PUBLIC WALKWAY; *BELOW*:CROSS SECTION OF CATALOGUE ROOM

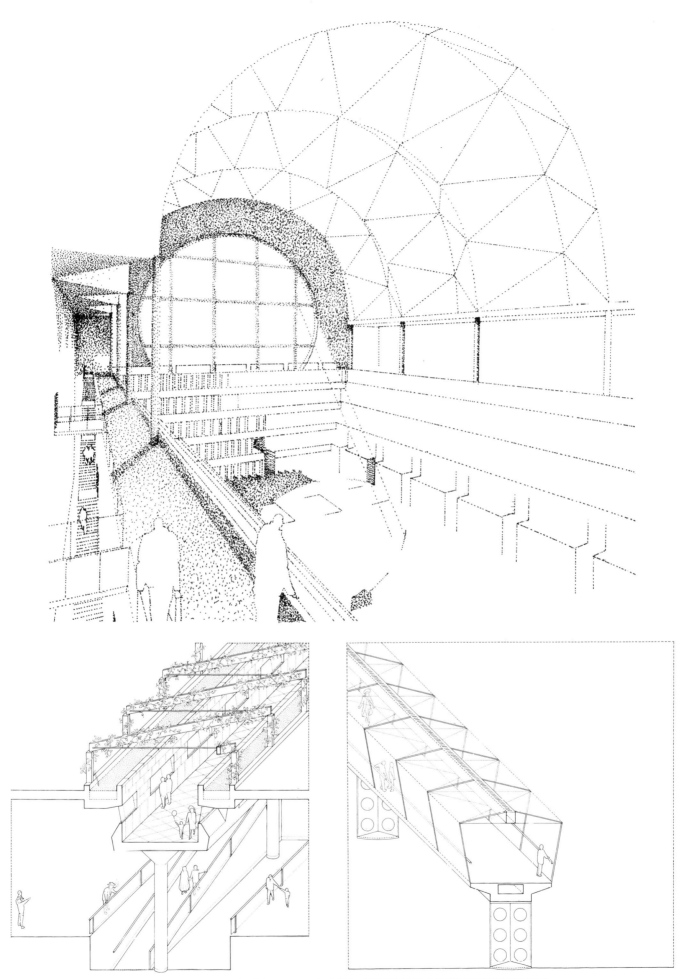

ABOVE: REFERENCE LIBRARY *BELOW L TO R*: PUBLIC WALKWAYS OVER AND THROUGH THE BUILDING

ABOVE L TO R: CROSS SECTIONS; *CENTRE L TO R*: ELEVATIONS; *BELOW*: LONGITUDINAL SECTION

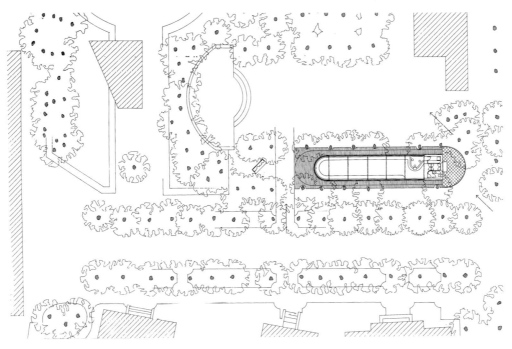

ABOVE: SITE PLAN; *BELOW*: ELEVATION

BIENNALE BOOKSHOP
VENICE

The bookship-boatshop is located close to the new Italian pavilion, in a strategic position, between the avenues of trees bordering the main public footpath. Overhanging eaves project over the boardwalk which runs around the three glazed sides of the bookshop. The roof creates a continuous awning above the shop window. Books will be laid out flat for browsing and window display along a 40m timber bench top, and stored below the bench in 'honeycomb' metal shelving units. Roof trusses support a central duct carrying airconditioning, lighting, alarm systems etc.

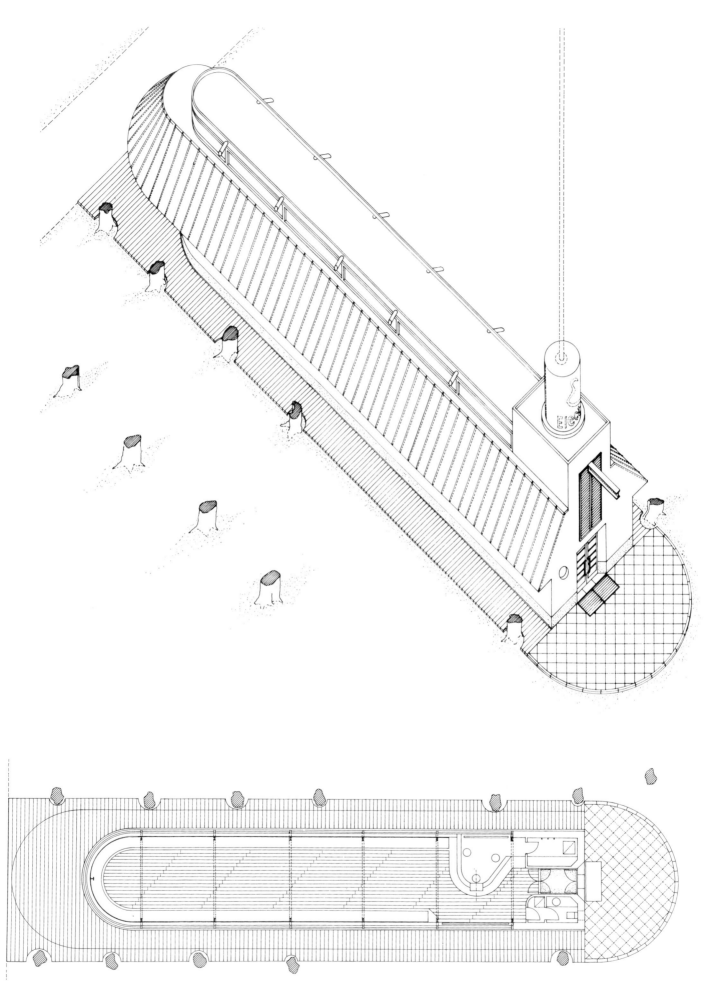

ABOVE: AXONOMETRIC: *BELOW*: FLOOR PLAN

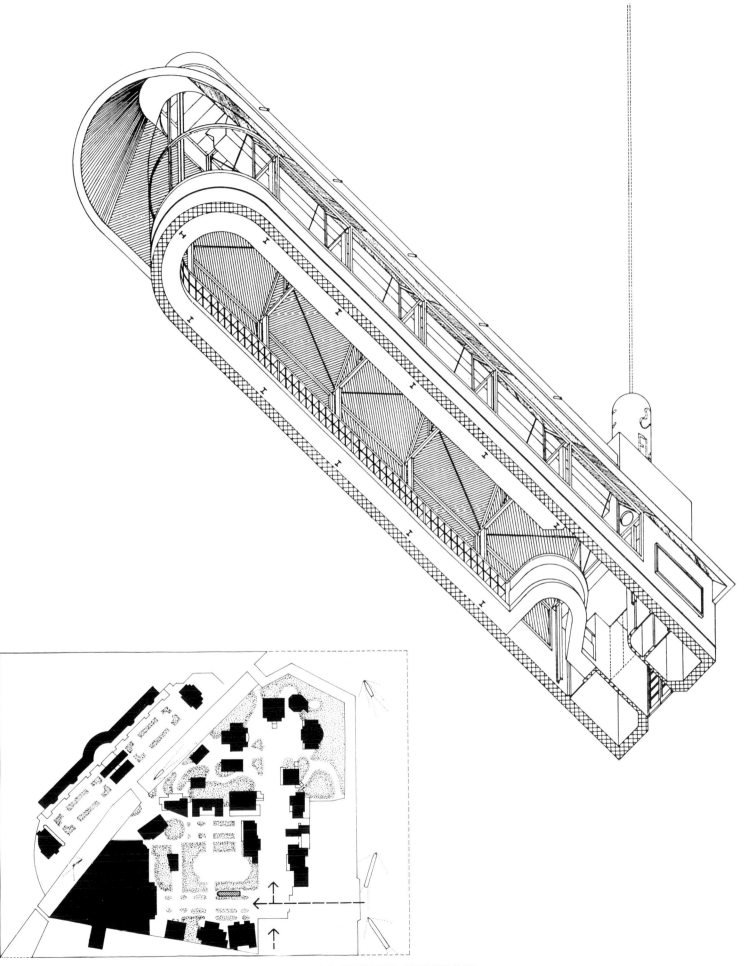

ABOVE: WORM'S AXONOMETRIC; *BELOW*: SITE PLAN

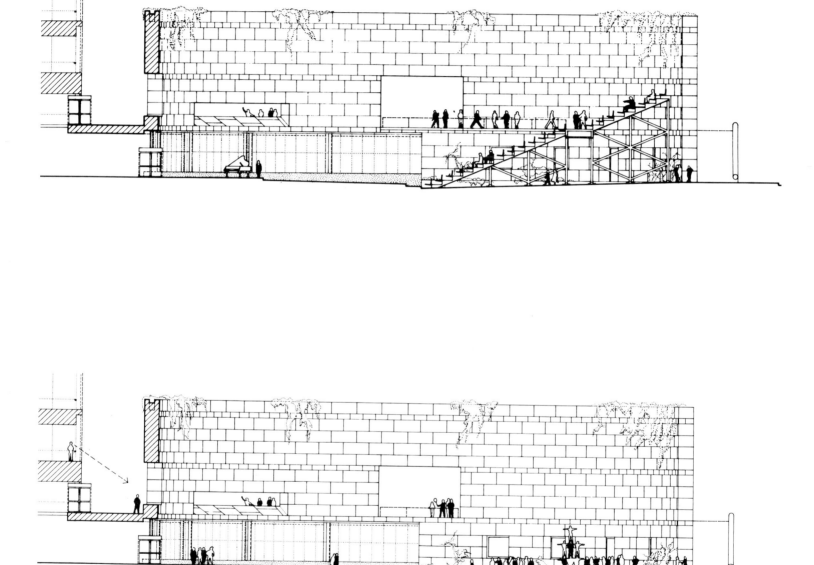

CIRCULAR COURTYARD SECTION, WITH AND WITHOUT FLEXIBLE SEATING

ABOVE: ROOF PLAN; *BELOW*: MODEL PHOTOGRAPH

TOKYO INTERNATIONAL FORUM
TOKYO

Our proposal for the Tokyo International Forum emphasises the symbolic importance of the complex by placing a tall building in the centre and relating it to the outdoor public place. Lower, but equally monumental buildings are placed on each side providing long façades to Road 406 and Ward Road. A towering centrepiece surrounded by identifiable elements is in the 20th-century tradition of 'Stadtkrone' or 'city crown'. The allusion can be extended to the transparency of the buildings, which is both an interpretation of 'Glasarchitektur', and an expression of the new building and servicing technologies in an age when energy conservation is critical. Searchlights, lasers and 'fantastic' components contribute to this association. The transparent buildings are placed on a sandstone base which encloses the most publicly accessible areas of the complex. The base can be considered either as a traditional counterpart to the 'technological' structures above it or as a hill with approach paths to the 'city crown'. The circular courtyard forms part of the base and is enclosed by a wall of stone. This wall has large window openings allowing views from the upper terraces to the activity below.

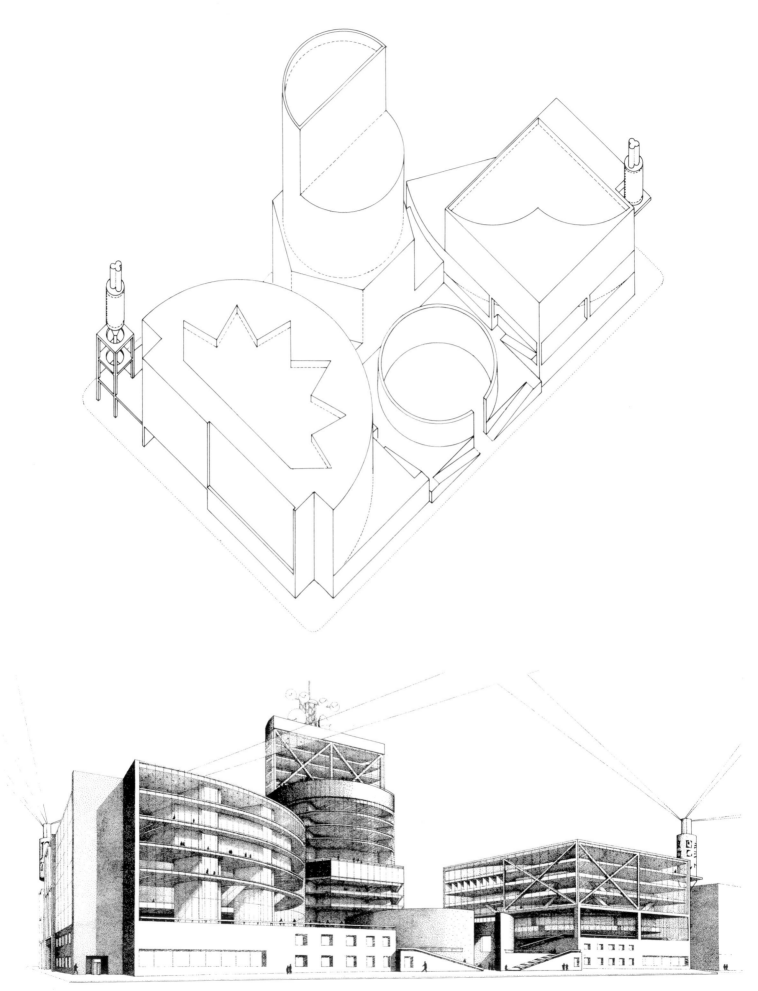

ABOVE: AXONOMETRIC; *BELOW*: PERSPECTIVE VIEW FROM NORTH

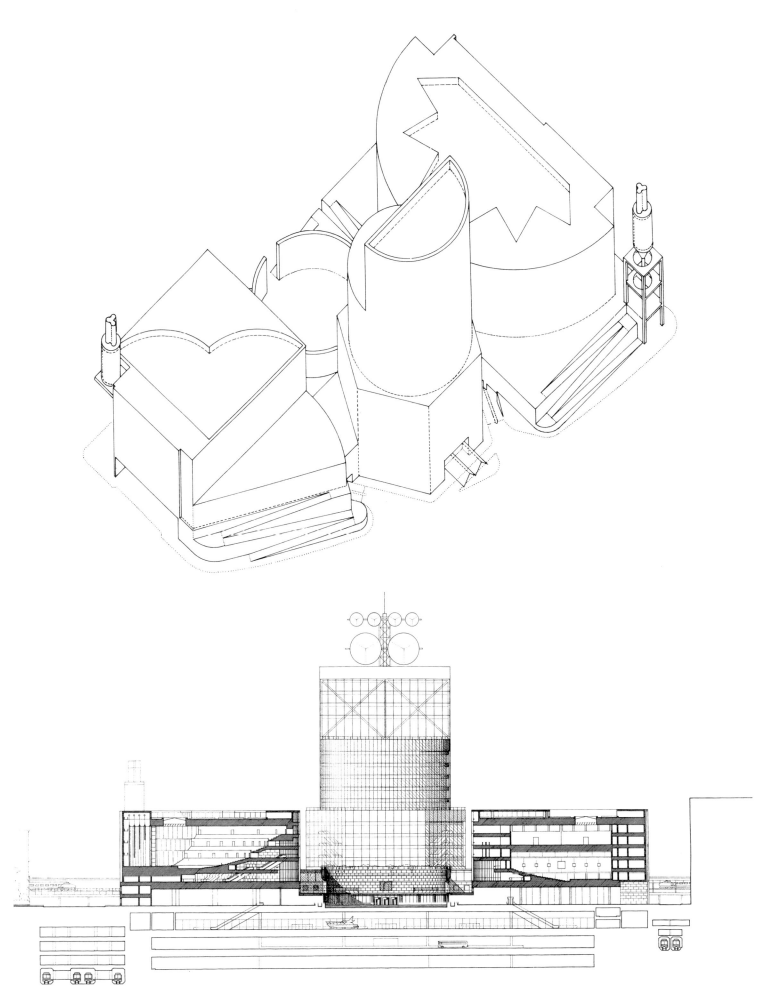

ABOVE: AXONOMETRIC; *BELOW*: CROSS SECTION

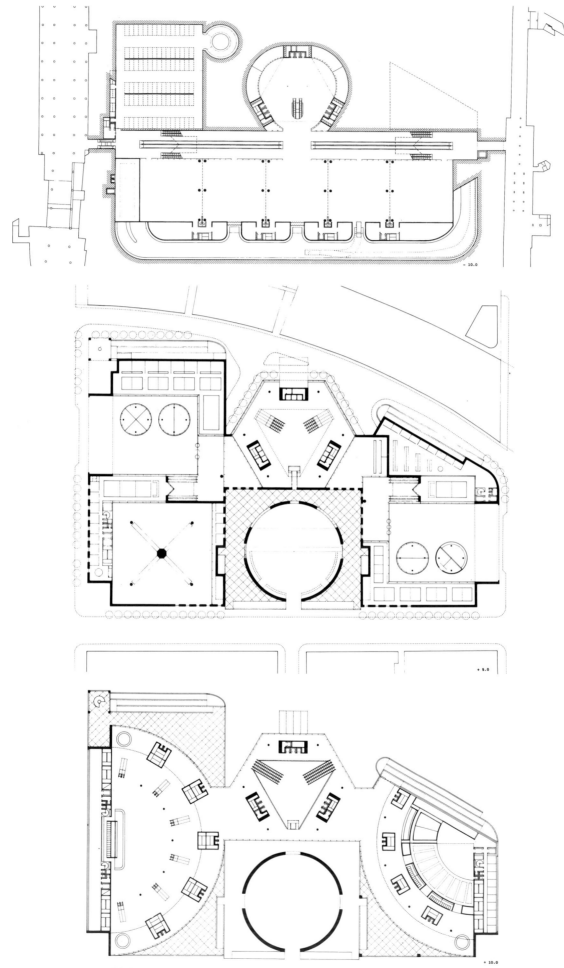

ABOVE: BASEMENT LEVEL PLAN; *CENTRE*: GROUND LEVEL PLAN; *BELOW*: FIRST LEVEL PLAN

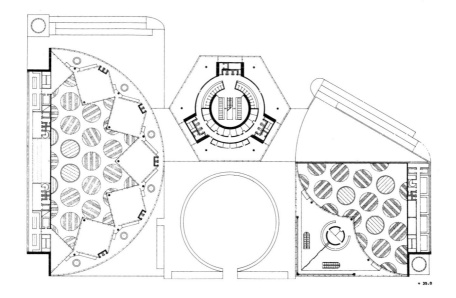

+ 35.0

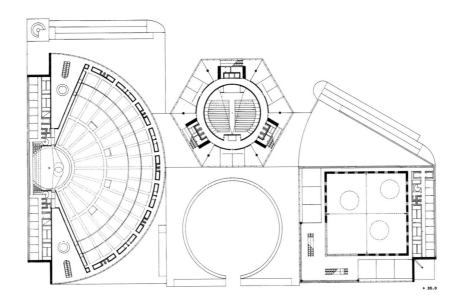

+ 30.0

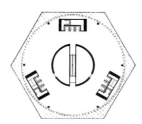

ABOVE: UPPER LEVEL PLAN; *CENTRE*: HIGH LEVEL PLAN; *BELOW L TO R*: HIGH LEVEL TOWER PLANS

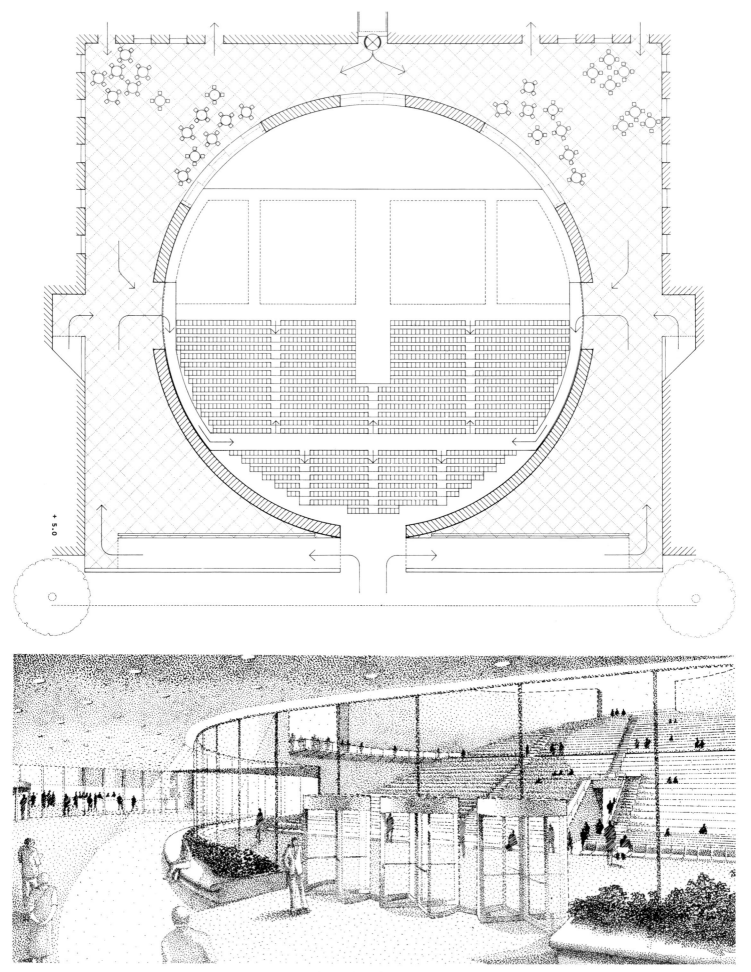

ABOVE: CIRCULAR COURTYARD SEATING PLAN; *BELOW*: INTERIOR PERSPECTIVE VIEW

+ 5.0

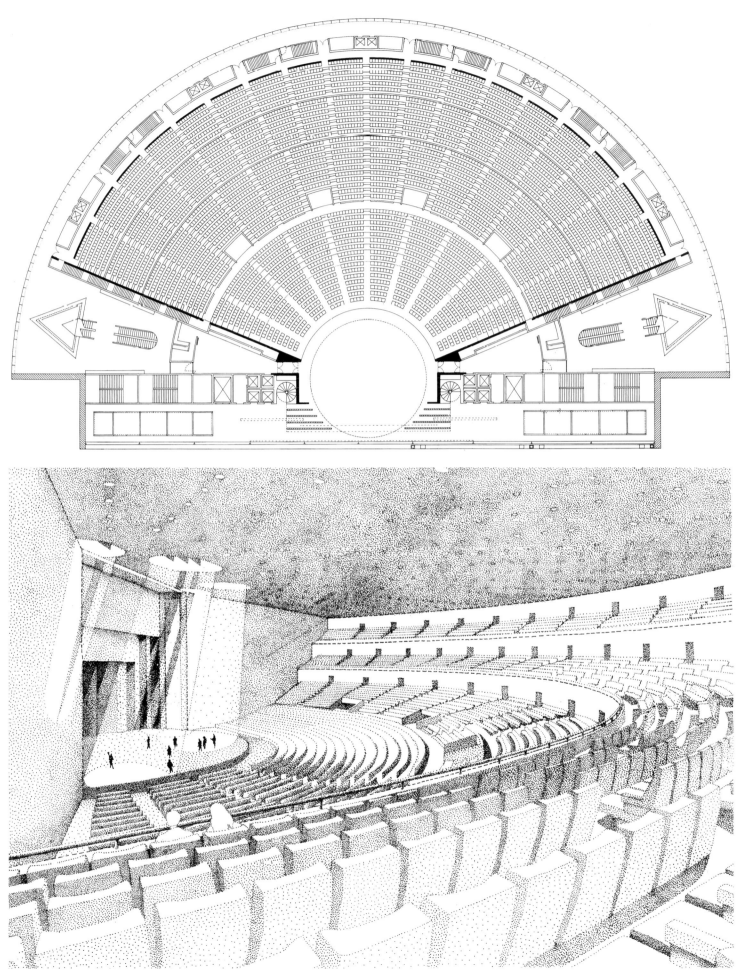

ABOVE: AUDITORIUM SEATING PLAN; *BELOW:* AUDITORIUM PERSPECTIVE

CURRICULUM VITAE

JAMES STIRLING

PERSONAL
Born 1926, Glasgow. Family moved to Liverpool in 1927. Married 1966. One son, two daughters.

EDUCATION
Quarry Bank High School, Liverpool until 1941.
Liverpool School of Art, 1942.
Liverpool University, School of Architecture, 1945-1950, Dipl. Arch. (dist.). (Student Exchange to New York, USA).
School of Town Planning and Regional Research, London, 1950-1952.

DESIGN AND PROFESSIONAL EXPERIENCE
Private Practice from 1956 (Partners: James Gowan until 1963, Michael Wilford from 1971).

TEACHING EXPERIENCE
Visiting Teacher at Architectural Association, London, 1957. Regent Street Polytechnic, London, 1958-1960.
Cambridge University, School of Architecture, 1961. Visiting Critic at Yale University School of Architecture, USA, 1960, 1962. RIBA External Examiner for Architectural Education at the Bartlett (London University) 1968-1971. Also Regent Street Polytechnic from 1965.
Charles Davenport Visiting Professor Yale University School of Architecture USA 1967-1984. Professor, Düsseldorf Kunstakademie from 1977.
Bannister Fletcher Professor, London University, 1977. Architectural Association External Examiner, London 1979-81.

GENERAL
Honorary Member of the Akademie der Künste, Berlin from 1969. BBC/Arts Council Film: 'James Stirling's Architecture', 1973. 'James Stirling Building and Projects, 1950-1974', Thames and Hudson, 1975.
Honorary Fellow of the American Institute of Architects, from 1976. Brunner Award, National Institute of Arts and Letters, USA, 1976. Alvar Aalto award, Helsinki, 1977.
Honorary Member of the Florence Academy of Arts, 1979. Honorary Doctorate, Royal College of Art, 1979. Fellow of the Royal Society of Arts, London, 1979. Honorary Member of the Accademia Nazionale, San Luca, Italy, 1979.
RIBA Royal Gold Medal for Architecture, London, 1980. Pritzker Prize, 1981. Architect in Residence, American Academy in Rome, 1982.
Honorary Member, Bund Deutscher Architekten, 1983.
Associate RA (Royal Academy, London), 1985.
Chicago Architecture Award, 1985.
Thomas Jefferson Medal (USA) 1986.
James Stirling BBC and International Film by Michael Blackwood 1987.
Hugo Haring Prize, Germany, 1988.
Honorary Member, American Institute of Arts and Letters, 1990.

EXHIBITIONS
James Stirling – Three Buildings Exhibition at MoMA. New York, 1969.
James Stirling – Drawings Exhibition at RIBA Gallery, London 1974.
19 Projects – Travelling Exhibition (initiated by Naples University 1975 and British Council): Naples, Rome, Brussels, Zurich, Lausanne, Tehran, Trieste etc. Dortmund '9 Architects' Exhibition, Dortmund University, 1976. Venice Biennale, July 1976.
Via Arte Della Lana, Sanmichele, Florence, 1977.
'Architecture l'– Leo Castelli Gallery, New York, 1977.
Roma Interrotta, Rome, 1978.
'Museum Projects' Exhibition Dortmund University, 1979. Exhibition 'Manhattan Townhouses' New York, 1980.
RIBA Exhibition '3 German Projects' London, 1980.
Drawings of the new extension, Fogg Museum, Cambridge Mass, USA, 1981.
'10 New Buildings' Exhibition at ICA. London, 1983.
'Model Futures' Exhibition at I.C.A. London, 1983.
PAC, Cornell University, Architectural League, New York, 1984.

Wissenschaftszentrum, Berlin, 1985.
Royal Academy, London 1986. British Architecture - Foster, Rogers, Stirling. Tate Gallery. Stirling and Wilford's Tate Museums, London and Liverpool 1987.

PUBLICATIONS
James Stirling, Drawings Exhibition catalogue, RIBA Drawings Collection 1974
James Stirling, Buildings and Projects, James Stirling, Michael Wilford and Associates, Rizzoli, New York, 1984.
James Stirling, Die Neue Staatsgalerie, Stuttgart, V G Hatje, Stuttgart, 1984.
'Stirling since Stuttgart', *A + U* November 1986, The Japan Architect Co. Ltd.
Clore Gallery for the Turner Collection, Tate Gallery, London, (catalogue) 1987.
The Arthur M Sackler Museum, Harvard University, (catalogue) 1987

MICHAEL JAMES WILFORD

PERSONAL
Born 1938, Surbiton, Surrey, England. Married 1960. Two sons and three daughters. Resident London, England.

EDUCATION
Kingston Technical School, 1950-1955.
Northern Polytechnic School of Architecture, London 1955-1962. Honours Diploma with Distinction in Thesis (Buildings for Secondary Education). Regent Street Polytechnic Planning School, London 1967.

PROFESSIONAL EXPERIENCE
Senior Assistant with James Stirling and James Gowan 1960-1963.
Senior Assistant with James Stirling 1963-1965.
Associate Partner with James Stirling 1965-1971.
Partner with James Stirling from 1971.

TEACHING EXPERIENCE
Visiting Critic, Yale University School of Architecture, USA, 1968 and 1975.
Juror, Harvard University School of Architecture, USA, 1968.
Juror, Washington University School of Architecture, USA, 1968. Tutor Architectural Association, London, 1969-1973.
Visiting Critic, Sheffield University School of Architecture, UK, 1974-1979.
Visiting Critic, Toronto University School of Architecture, Canada, 1974-1983.
Visiting Critic, McGill University School of Architecture, Montreal, 1975.
Visiting Critic, & Tutor, Rice University, Houston, USA, 1978 and 1979.
Visiting Professor, Rice University School of Architecture, Houston, 1980-1988.
Graham Willis Visiting Professor in Architecture, Sheffield University School of Architecture, UK, 1980-1988.
External Examiner, Royal College of Art School of Enviromental Design, London, 1978 and 1979.
External Examiner, Polytechnic of North London, 1983-1986.
External Examiner, Leeds Polytechnic School of Architecture, 1983-1985.
External Examiner, PCL. School of Architecture, 1986-1989.
Royal Institute of British Architects, London Region Masterclass, 1988.
External Examiner, Bartlett School of Architecture, London, 1989 -1992.
Visiting Fellow, University of Newcastle, New South Wales, Australia, 1989.

GENERAL
Member of the Royal Institute of British Architects Education and Professional Development Committee, 1979-1981.
Jury Member, AIA. Minnesota Annual Architectural Design Awards 1979.
Assessor Architectural Competition for Oriental Art Museum, Durham University, England, 1982.
Chairman Assessor, Royal Institute of British Architects, Architecture Awards, Welsh Region 1987.
Hugo Haring Prize, Germany, 1988.
Assessor, Eternit 8th International Architecture Prize, Brussels 1988.
Honorary Doctorate, Sheffield University, 1989.
Chairman Assessor, Royal Institute of British Architects Architecture Awards Yorkshire Region 1989.